D0966701

WOMEN OF COURAGE

By Margaret Truman

Women of Courage
Harry S. Truman
White House Pets
Souvenir

WOMEN
OF
COURAGE

by Margaret Truman

WILLIAM MORROW AND COMPANY, INC.
NEW YORK   1976

Copyright © 1976 by Margaret Truman Daniel

All rights reserved. No part of this book may be reproduced or utilized in any form or by any means, electronic or mechanical, including photocopying, recording or by any information storage and retrieval system, without permission, in writing from the Publisher. Inquiries should be addressed to William Morrow and Company, Inc., 105 Madison Ave., New York, N. Y. 10016.

Printed in the United States of America.

1   2   3   4   5   80   79   78   77   76

Library of Congress Cataloging in Publication Data

Truman, Margaret (date)
  Women of courage.

  Includes index.
  SUMMARY: Brief biographies emphasizing the courage of twelve women both famous and little-known in United States history.
    1. Women—United States—Biography.   [1. United States—Biography]
I. Title.
CT3260.T79   920.72   [920]   75-45456
ISBN 0-688-03038-6

For my mother
who is definitely a woman of courage

Acknowledgments

I would like to thank Dr. Alan M. Fern, Chief, Prints and Photographs Division, Library of Congress, for his help in discovering some rare pictures of these women of courage. My secretary, Fifi Edison, has also been very helpful in the search for these pictures, as well as in the preparation of the manuscript. I would like to extend my special thanks to Mrs. Alfreda M. B. Duster for sending me a rare photograph of her mother, Ida Wells-Barnett. Finally, I am grateful to Alice and Thomas Fleming for their expert assistance in researching and organizing this book.

Contents

WOMEN OF COURAGE

Women and Courage

When Elizabeth Cady Stanton first proposed that women should begin working for the right to vote, her father was so upset that he made a special visit to her home in Seneca Falls, New York, to see if she had suffered a mental breakdown. He was relieved to see that she was still sane but he could not reconcile himself to her strange behavior. "My child," he told her, "I wish you had waited until I was under the sod before you had done this foolish thing."

That was back in 1848. Even in our own century, the woman who dares to set her sights on new horizons is apt to be regarded as slightly demented. Nevertheless, our history books and encyclopedias are filled with the names of women who have taken this risk. Some of them faced the alienation of family and friends, others renounced comforts and pleasures that could have been theirs for the asking. All of them endured criticism that, for sheer viciousness and cruelty, went far beyond anything that was heaped on men. Where did they find the strength? I believe it emerged from a heritage of courage that was already two hundred years old when Elizabeth Cady Stanton faced her frowning father.

In recent years, we have heard a lot about women

accepting new challenges, carving out new roles, pushing for equality in every aspect of their lives. I have followed their progress and admired their perseverance, but their efforts have, at the same time, prompted me to take a closer look at the outstanding women in our past. There are an extraordinary number of them—doctors, writers, educators, scientists—but among these hundreds of distinguished women, there is a smaller group in whom I believe today's women can take special pride—the women of courage.

Courage is sometimes defined as the quality of mind and spirit that enables a person to meet danger, difficulty or pain with firmness. There are at least a half dozen varieties of courage. *Bravery* is daring and defiant; *heroism,* noble and self-sacrificing; *fortitude,* patient and persevering. American women have shown them all.

In this book, I have chosen twelve women who illustrate my thoughts and beliefs about courage. They range from an Indian squaw to a United States senator, from an Irish immigrant to the daughter of slaves to a First Lady. Most of them wore bonnets and ankle-length skirts, few had college degrees, and only a handful ever stepped into a voting booth. When it came to courage, however, these women not only spoke the same language as their sisters of today, but more often than not their voices came through in stronger, clearer tones.

My look into the past has taught me several things about the tradition of feminine courage in the United States. Like almost everything else in history, it has been an evolving experience. We can see its roots in the seventeenth and eighteenth centuries, in the physical courage that the first American women needed to confront the treacherous Atlantic and the equally harrowing wilderness.

William Bradford, the Pilgrim leader, summed it up in the terse, heartbreaking words of his history of the Plymouth Colony's first terrible year: "But that which was most sad and lamentable was that in two or three months time, half of their company dyed, especially in January and February, being the depth of winter and wanting houses and other comforts, being infected with the scurvy and other diseases which this long voyage . . . had brought upon them."

Along with the constant threat of death from disease and starvation, the first settlers also had to contend with the danger of Indians. An entire literature has been written by and about pioneer women who were captured by Indians and survived only by enduring the same brutal physical hardships that their captors accepted as a matter of course.

In Massachusetts, forty-year-old Hannah Duston saw her week-old infant smashed against a tree. She was then forced to make a winter march of over one hundred miles in her bare feet. A Pennsylvania teenager, Mary Jemison, witnessed the massacre of her father, mother, sister, and two brothers. Yet these women and the others who came after them found within themselves the strength to overcome despair, humiliation, exhaustion.

In our own era, when women are taking jobs as police officers and Secret Service agents, jockeys and steeplejacks, women's physical courage has become a subject for public debate. The skeptics who belittle the female ability to handle such roles obviously never heard of heroines like Margaret Corbin, who helped fire her husband's cannon during the British attack on New York in 1776. Or Nancy Hart, who trapped five Loyalist marauders in her cabin on Georgia's Broad River, shot one dead, mortally wounded another, and took the remaining three captive.

This tradition of physical courage has asserted itself throughout our history. It sustained those tens of thousands of nameless pioneer women who walked and rode beside their men in the hundred years that Americans surged westward to conquer a continent. It burned within runaway slaves like Harriet Tubman, a "conductor" on the famous Underground Railroad, who smuggled some three hundred black men and women across the Mason-Dixon line to freedom. Beyond question, it was the inspiration for Amelia Earhart, who electrified the world with her daring long-distance flights in the 1930s.

In the decades after the American Revolution, the frontier gradually moved away from the Atlantic coastline and eventually disappeared. During this same period, the changing circumstances of their lives forced American women to begin evolving another tradition of courage. It was a special blend of physical and moral tenacity with an element of the personal that male courage in similar areas often lacked.

American women needed this second kind of courage because of a peculiar shift in the nation's social and economic attitudes. In colonial days, women enjoyed a surprising amount of independence—an essential ingredient of courage. Women with property voted regularly in New England town meetings, and one forthright female, Margaret Brent, even demanded a seat in the Maryland legislature. Before the American Revolution, no fewer than twelve newspapers were being published by women in various towns along the eastern seaboard. In New York, Dutch women imported and exported, owned shops and ships, and built up independent fortunes. In the South, women ran plantations. One, Eliza Pinckney, after five years of experimentation, succeeded in growing indigo—a crop that had already been tried and abandoned by male planters—and made it one of South Carolina's most important exports.

In diaries and letters, we catch vivid glimpses of these remarkable colonial women. William Byrd of Virginia described one he met in the back country: "She is a very civil woman and shews nothing of ruggedness or Immodesty in her carriage, yett she will carry a gunn in the woods and kill deer, turkeys, etc., shoot down wild cattle, catch and ty hoggs, knock down beeves with an ax and perform manfull Exercises as well as most men in these parts."

The independence of colonial women was created by necessity as much as by choice. The men who set out to tame a wilderness and develop a continent welcomed all the help they could get, and they were not inclined to quibble about whether their helpers wore skirts or breeches. There was, in addition, a strong dislike of idleness, particularly among religious New Englanders, that reinforced this attitude.

Colonial women had every reason to believe that their status would not only continue but would be improved by the American Revolution. Abigail Adams made this very clear in a letter to her congressman husband, John.

In the new code of laws which I suppose it will be necessary for you to make [she wrote], I desire you would remember the ladies and be more generous and favorable to them than your ancestors. Do not put such unlimited power into the hands of the husbands. Remember all men would be tyrants if they could. If particular care and attention is not paid to the ladies, we are determined to foment a rebellion, and will not hold ourselves bound by any laws in which we have no voice or representation.

Unfortunately, Abigail Adams's high hopes and bold threats both came to naught. The great surge toward equality that had been a natural part of life in the thirteen colonies was already on its way to extinction by the time George Washington ended his second term as President of the United States.

One reason was an abrupt change in the political

and social climate. The free-wheeling optimism of the eighteenth century was swept aside by the flood of conformity and reaction that engulfed both England and the United States in the wake of the French Revolution. Ironically, it was a woman, Queen Victoria, who gave her name to the long period of prudery and social repression that began a few decades later.

At the same time, the Industrial Revolution was gradually ushering in an age in which men worked not in their own homes or in shops adjacent to those homes, but in factories some distance away. Their wives, no longer able to pitch in and help when needed, were left to their duties as homemakers and mothers.

But the most significant ingredient in the male prejudice that surrounded American women of the nineteenth century was the country's growing sense of self-importance. Once the republic had been launched, Americans turned their attention to becoming a respected and civilized nation. In the process, they took to aping their former masters, the British.

In England, the ideal of the lady was not only enshrined among the upper classes, it was equally revered by the middle and lower classes, who had an almost ridiculous awe of wealth and social position. A lady was supposed to lavish her attention on her clothes and coiffure and spend her time organizing or attending banquets and balls. She was educated (*trained* would be a better word) in music, needlework, and polite conversation. She was never supposed to be concerned with politics or business, and she was certainly not allowed to soil her hands or tax her mind with anything as strenuous as work.

A distressing number of American men and, I'm sorry to say, quite a few of their women, completely accepted the English attitude toward ladies. They might have had a hard time inflicting it on the rest of the United States but for one peculiar fact. The new country was becoming rich.

As a woman historian, Elizabeth Anthony Dexter, put it, "It seems to be a law of life that as people become prosperous they desire to multiply their luxuries and . . . of all luxuries one of the most coveted is the possession of 'ladies,' a class of women, that is, who reflect credit upon their husbands and fathers in exact proportion to their uselessness."

In the first fifty years of the nineteenth century, the American woman actually lost ground in the face of this smother-them-with-silks-and-satins offensive. Pampered into a state of semi-, and sometimes total, dependence, she was forbidden to do anything that might jeopardize her status as a lady.

When the nineteenth-century novelist and antislavery writer, Lydia Maria Child, published her first book, she later recalled, "I was gravely warned by some of my female acquaintances that no woman could expect to be regarded as a lady after she had written a book."

The social conventions that conspired to keep women in a state of voluntary subjugation soon crystallized into hard and fast rules. As our society became more sophisticated, the concept of training for a whole range of trades and professions developed. Women were systematically excluded from such opportunities. It had become an accepted fact that they were neither physically nor psychologically equipped to handle them.

A further menace to feminine freedom was the codification of laws, which became almost a mania as Americans strove to prove that they were just as civilized as the rest of the world. Reflecting the tenor of the times, the lawmakers routinely deprived women of some of the basic rights that had previously been theirs. One glaring example is suffrage.

Traditionally, women did not vote, but most states had no laws forbidding them from exercising the franchise. One by one, even the more liberal states began to change their laws. The lone holdout was New Jersey. Then, in 1807, a Garden State politician bent on winning a local election marshaled a battalion of female supporters and led them to the polls. Their ballots tipped the scales in his favor, but the election prompted the state legislature to make New Jersey the final state to bar women from the political process.

It is a tribute to feminine courage that, despite the restrictions imposed on them in the nineteenth century, American women continued to distinguish themselves. There was, however, a new ingredient in their experience. Women who sought distinction outside of the home and marriage did so with the knowledge that they were moving against the grain of their society. They faced a new and, in many ways, more formidable test of their courage.

Physical courage was by no means a relic of the past. The women who demanded the right to vote and to join the professions often faced physical violence from male mobs. Their sisters in the fight against slavery and the battle for fair labor laws were threatened by bricks, clubs, and bullets. But the moral challenges were much more formidable.

Shortly after he was elected to the Senate, President John F. Kennedy wrote his inspiring book, *Profiles in Courage*. In it, he told the stories of a group of senators who had the courage to put aside personal and political considerations and do what they thought was best for the nation. I would be the last person in the world to denigrate political courage. Nor can I disagree with Kennedy's con-tention—made over twenty years ago but still valid—that the challenge of political courage looms larger now than ever before.

But John F. Kennedy's heroes were men who had a considerable amount of power and prestige to bolster their courage and a political base from which to operate. By and large, the American women who have chosen to oppose the establishment stood alone or, at best, with only a few followers behind them.

The men who espoused unpopular causes may have been considered misguided, but they were rarely attacked for their morals or their masculinity. Women who did the same thing were apt to be denounced as harlots or condemned for being *unfeminine*—an all-purpose word that was used to describe almost any category of female behavior of which men disapproved.

Mounting a personal attack against an opponent instead of responding to his arguments has always been considered unfair when used against men. Against women, it became the standard response. Personal attacks were a handy way to distract public attention from what a woman was saying. They were especially convenient when she was saying something the majority of males did not want to hear. Behind the sneers lurked the most vicious prejudice of all —the conviction that women were social and intellectual inferiors.

When Emma Willard submitted a plan for improving female education to the New York State Legislature in 1818, a joke immediately began making the rounds—"Next thing you know they'll be educating cows."

Even after Mrs. Willard succeeded in persuading the legislators to grant a charter to her Waterford Academy for Young Ladies—the first official recognition of women's right to be educated—the skepticism persisted. When the schoolmistress invited the citizens of Waterford to attend a public examination at which one of her pupils recited theorems in geometry, the spectators stared in disbelief. "She must have memorized them," was the consensus. "No woman could possibly understand geometry."

The tendency to ridicule any woman with a serious purpose has persisted into our own era. Few women in modern times have been subjected to as much criticism as Eleanor Roosevelt. She was the butt of cruel jokes about everything from her appearance to her travels around the country. With the kind of quiet dignity that is so often a mark of a courageous woman, Eleanor Roosevelt rose above them all. The perpetrators of the jokes and the gossip have long since been forgotten, but Mrs. Roosevelt will always be remembered as a gracious and courageous lady.

A number of definitive biographies have already been written about Eleanor Roosevelt. There is little I can add to her story. Suffice it to say here that, in my opinion, she personifies the evolution of feminine courage from the physical to the moral plane. Perhaps more than anyone else, she has been the inspiration for the women of today.

As Eleanor Roosevelt amply demonstrated, courage is an affirmation of life. When we study it more closely, we also see that it is the affirmation of the *best* in life. It involves our values, our hopes, our dreams, all the things that are part of the struggle to make the world a better place.

My explorations into the lives of American women have taught me a number of other things about courage. It is rarely reckless or foolish. On the contrary, courage usually involves a highly realistic estimate of the odds that must be faced. Nor can the women who display courage be dismissed as mere showoffs. Quite the opposite. Most of the women I encountered in my research had no burning desire to tackle the jobs confronting them. Often they experienced agonies of self-doubt and were beset by anxiety and indecision.

In a scene from one of my favorite plays, *The Madwoman of Chaillot,* that dear delightful woman remarks, "Nothing is ever so wrong in the world that a sensible woman can't set it straight in the course of an afternoon." If only it were that simple!

The great moral crusades of the nineteenth century —every one of which was inspired or supported by women— took decades to win, and each required fantastic reserves of perseverance and strength simply to stay in the fight. These battles, however, seem almost brief in comparison to the fight for woman suffrage. The goal, first announced by Elizabeth Cady Stanton in 1848, was not achieved until 1920—seventy-two years later.

One of the most difficult things to accept about courage is that it does not automatically make a person attractive or lovable. Often it makes them just the opposite. Susan B. Anthony had a cantankerous disposition, a domineering nature, and an unswerving dedication to her goals—all of which made her an ideal candidate for leading the fight for the right to vote but also explain why many people, including some of her followers, considered her a pain in the neck. I admire Miss Anthony's courage, but I doubt that I would have chosen her as a friend.

Similarly, courageous people are not necessarily right all the time. There are women in this book whom I wholeheartedly applaud for their stands on one issue but with whom I strongly disagree on others. Kate Barnard waged many brave battles on behalf of Indian orphans, but I find it hard to forgive her opposition to woman suffrage. And the suffragists, who made perfect sense in their fight for equal rights at the polls, went completely off the track when they decided to support Prohibition.

The women I've chosen to write about had their quota of human failings and foibles just like the rest of us.

They also had the same bad habit of making mistakes. But they share one transcendent quality. All of them in some way, at some time, acted courageously. I hope their stories will give you, as they gave me, a fresh appreciation of women's contributions to America's past, a better insight into that complex virtue, courage, and above all, a vision of what women can do to improve the quality of our lives.

Part I

Courage and Crises

I have often wondered how women developed the reputation for being timid emotional creatures who can't be counted on in a crisis. American history abounds with stories of women who remained calm and decisive in any number of terrifying situations.

The simple fact is that the ingredients of this kind of courage—steady nerves, sound judgment, the ability to set aside fear—have never been exclusively masculine qualities. Nor have their opposites—panic, hysteria, and cowardice—ever been exclusively feminine.

Nevertheless, even those of us who have never accepted the popular stereotypes still feel a peculiar and perhaps inordinate sense of pride when a woman shows physical courage. Why? I used to think it was female chauvinism on my part until I realized that most men feel the same way. After further reflection, I concluded that if people make more of a fuss over feminine courage in a crisis, it is because the courage itself has an added dimension.

Ever since the days of the cavemen, males have been the acknowledged protectors of home, family, and country. It has always been assumed that they were by nature more adventurous and aggressive, more willing to risk their lives. Women, on the other hand, have had no such image to live up to. They were "the weaker sex" and it was perfectly all right for them to faint, or flee, or fail to act in a time of danger.

Thus it has been all the more surprising when a woman, who was not under any pressure to act heroically, chose to do so on her own. In almost every instance, she was going out of her way to take on a burden she could just as easily have avoided.

Commendable as this may seem to the rest of us, the women who displayed this kind of courage would probably be astonished that anyone should marvel at their actions. In the first place, most of them had neither the desire nor the temperament to play damsel in distress. More important, however, courage to them was not a question of sex or of social custom but of conscience. They had to deal with their crises courageously for one very good reason: they could not have lived with themselves if they had behaved in any other way.

Nightmare at Liberty Hall

My favorite heroine of the American Revolution is someone many people have never heard of—Susan Livingston. Susan had all of the qualities that are usually thought of as feminine. She was pretty and coquettish, fond of clothes, parties, and dancing. But when she found herself facing the most difficult crisis of her life, she proved without question that femininity can coexist quite comfortably with fearlessness.

I like Susan Livingston for several reasons. For one thing, she had a controversial politician for a father— William Livingston, the "rebel" Governor of New Jersey. For another, she lived in a big, comfortable house that she loved as much as I love my parents' old home in Independence.

The Livingston homestead, Liberty Hall, still stands and continues to be owned by Livingston descendants. It is a rambling three-story structure tucked behind a stone wall on a busy highway just outside of Elizabeth, New Jersey. When Susan Livingston lived there, the highway was no more than a dirt road, the house was surrounded by lush farmland, and Elizabeth was a small, sedate seaport known as Elizabethtown.

My father, I know, would have sympathized with William Livingston. Dad had only one daughter to cope with; Governor Livingston had three. They were known as the "Three Graces," and from all accounts they were as lively as they were lovely.

Susan, the Governor's middle daughter, was slightly less pretty than her sisters. She was also slightly less dignified, and had an unfortunate habit of frightening prospective suitors away with her devastating wit. In this and a number of other traits, Susan took after her father.

This meant she was naturally combative. William Livingston loved an argument. Before the Revolution, he turned New York and New Jersey upside-down as the leader of the opposition to a plan to import English bishops and set up an established Anglican Church in America. As a Presbyterian, he was inclined to think that the next step would be the elimination of religious freedom. He liked to call himself "The Primitive Whig," a man who had a love of freedom in his bones and was not afraid to risk everything for his beliefs. At the same time, he was an enormously affectionate man, a born father. He would leap up from a chair in his library, where he was often reading a book in Latin or French, and romp with his children like a five-year-old.

Susan's mother was an equally remarkable person. She was the calm, steadying influence in the family. She was also the money manager. In this department, the Governor was pretty close to inept. While he was busy fighting his religious and political battles, Mrs. Livingston, who was also named Susan, ran Liberty Hall and its 140-acre farm. She was more than able to hold her own as a separate and very independent personality, no small order in partnership with a man as volatile and dynamic as William Livingston.

LIBRARY OF CONGRESS

This is Liberty Hall, the house Susan Livingston defended against British and Loyalist raiders. It still stands on the outskirts of Elizabeth, N.J.

I suspect this combination of a capable mother and a father who was a born fighter had something to do with making Susan Livingston a courageous woman. Much as she admired her father, she remained very distinctly feminine, very consciously a woman. A constant visitor to Liberty Hall was Colonel Alexander Hamilton, who had a simplistic and derogatory opinion of women. He was also more than a little taken with himself as General Washington's youngest and most brilliant aide-de-camp. After a few sessions with the Livingston girls, he confessed in a letter to Susan's younger sister Kitty that a woman was "not a simple but a most complex, intricate and enigmatical being."

No leader of the Revolution except George Washington had a more difficult task than the Governor of New Jersey. The state was split almost fifty-fifty between Loyalists and rebels. Morale was a constant problem. Thousands gave up the fight and signed secret agreements with the British to remain neutral in return for a "protection." Others took advantage of the chaos to loot and abuse their neighbors. Still others concentrated on getting rich. In the middle of the war, Livingston wrote to Washington: "I am so discouraged by our public mismanagement & the additional load of business thrown upon me by the villainy of those who pursue nothing but accumulating fortunes to the ruin of their country that I almost sink under it."

But there was also an indomitable quality to this primitive Whig. "I have never desponded," he wrote another friend. "But I know at the same time that Providence will abandon us as a parcel of ingrates if we neglect to do for ourselves what we can do."

"To do for ourselves what we can do." That is a good definition of courage. Governor William Livingston lived it throughout the Revolution. So did his wife and daughters.

Liberty Hall was in no-man's-land. The British and Loyalists held New York, Long Island, and Staten Island, which was separated from Elizabethtown by a tiny strip of water known as "The Sound." On almost any night they chose to do so, British raiders could cross this swift-running stream and roam through the town almost at will. Their goal, more often than not, was the capture of some well-known patriot, who was then dragged back to New York and thrown into a British army prison.

Number One on the royal kidnap list was Governor William Livingston. Knowing this, the Governor seldom spent a night at Liberty Hall. He switched his sleeping quarters from one friend's house to another's on an impromptu, erratic schedule that made it difficult for anyone to betray him. This left Susan, the other unmarried Livingston daughter Kitty, their mother, and a handful of servants alone in the big mansion.

Governor Livingston worried about leaving his family unprotected and several times tried to persuade them to move to a safer location farther inland. All three women saw the anguish in his eyes when he made this proposal. Abandoned, Liberty Hall would almost certainly be looted and destroyed by the British or their Loyalist allies. No, they told him firmly, they would stay at Liberty Hall and take their chances. The Governor would ride off to Trenton to do battle with the legislature, worrying aloud but secretly relieved. He loved Liberty Hall, and it would have broken his heart to see it a charred ruin.

One evening in the spring of 1779, the British received word from one of their spies in New Jersey that Governor Livingston would be spending the night at Liberty Hall. The British commander on Staten Island, Brigadier Thomas Stirling, immediately decided to go after him.

At midnight, the Livingston women were awakened

by an angry pounding on their front door. Susan rushed to the window and stared out at an awesome sight. No less than a thousand British troops with fixed bayonets surrounded the house. Every few feet the ranks were illuminated by the glow of a torch held high to make sure that their quarry could not possibly escape.

Fortunately, the British had been given the wrong information. William Livingston was not at Liberty Hall. Susan elected herself to take charge in his absence. Turning to her mother and sister, she told them to remain upstairs. Then she put on a brightly flowered nightrobe and calmly descended to admit the British officer and his staff.

"Miss," said Brigadier Stirling with a stiff bow, "your father, the Governor, is in the house. For his own safety we trust he will surrender to us without resistance."

With unconcealed triumph, Susan told the Brigadier he had been misinformed. "My father seldom spends the night here," she said. "I fear you have gone to a great deal of trouble for nothing."

"She's lying," snarled an officer on the Brigadier's staff.

Stirling nodded. "We will have to search the house," he snapped.

"Go right ahead," Susan replied coolly.

At this point, their conversation was interrupted by the distant boom of a cannon. The sound came from the west. In that same instant, a pillar of flame blazed on Hobart Mountain, the highest point in the Short Hills, some six miles inland. It was the alarm gun and signal tower calling the local militia out to attack the British invaders.

If the Brigadier recognized the sound, he gave no sign. He barked some orders to his aides, and several squads of redcoats were soon swarming through Liberty Hall. One detachment stomped down the cellar stairs to search the kitchen and the servants' dining room, another prowled through the upstairs bedrooms, terrifying Mrs. Livingston and Kitty.

Ten minutes of furious searching produced no Governor. At least one officer expressed his rage and frustration by hacking at the lovely mahogany banister with his sword, leaving scars that are still visible today.

The alarm gun on Hobart Mountain continued to boom. As the Brigadier well knew, this part of New Jersey could muster two or three thousand militia. At this very moment the men might be on the road to Elizabethtown. But Thomas Stirling was a stubborn man. He did not intend to lose a night's sleep and embarrass himself before his troops by returning empty-handed. "If we cannot bring back the Governor," he declared, "we must at least have the pleasure of perusing his private papers."

"They aren't here," Susan solemnly assured him. "He carries most of them with him in a small trunk. The rest are in Trenton."

This was a bold-faced lie. The Governor's papers were only a few steps away in a locked secretary. If the British found them, they would obtain priceless information about the state of the Revolution in New Jersey. They would be fascinated to learn, for instance, the detailed orders for mustering the militia and their places of rendezvous. Even juicier would be the lists of persons exempt from the strict prohibition against traveling to New York. These lists were in George Washington's handwriting. Those named were spies, and if the British should learn their identities they would end up on the gallows.

The alarm gun still boomed, and from the distance came the faint sound of popping musketry. The militia were already skirmishing with the British pickets. Brigadier Stirling stormed out of the house to put his men in battle formation. His staff followed, leaving a major in charge of the search for Governor Livingston's papers.

The officer began methodically poking into every cabinet and chest in sight. Susan Livingston watched non-committally until he reached her father's secretary. Suddenly, she stepped in front of the major and in a voice aquiver with emotion begged him to leave the desk shut.

"In here," she said, placing her hand gently on the secretary's slanted top, "are letters that I have exchanged with a certain gentleman. If *you* are a gentleman, sir, you will not disturb them."

Like all British officers, the major prided himself on being a gentleman. He had no choice but to assure the winsome young rebel that he would not dream of touching her love letters. "But in exchange," he insisted, "you must show me where your father's papers are."

There were more popping sounds in the distance as the militia grew bolder. An officer rushed to the door to urge the major to hurry.

"Now, Miss Livingston, tell me," he commanded impatiently.

"All right," replied Susan with her sweetest smile, "I will. It's the least I can do for a *gentleman*."

She allowed the major to follow her back into the study, where she mounted the ladder to the upper shelves of the bookcases and began hauling down batches of papers. In a performance that would have done credit to an accomplished actress, Susan bitterly reproached herself for betraying her father's trust. The major tried to console her by pointing out that he probably would have found the papers anyway. Then he hastily handed them to his men, who stuffed the papers into their forage bags.

A brisk rattle of musketry shook the house. If they did not leave soon, the British would find themselves fighting a pitched battle with the gathering militiamen. Bowing his thanks to his ostensibly guilt-stricken hostess, the major rushed out the door and joined Brigadier Stirling and the rest of the troops for the boat ride back to Staten Island.

Toward dawn, the major proudly opened the forage bags in the Brigadier's quarters. The entire staff was on hand to gloat over the biggest intelligence coup of the war. But instead of Governor Livingston's private papers, the redcoats found themselves staring at several dozen sheafs of old law briefs dating back to the 1750s, when William Livingston had been one of the busiest attorneys in New York.

It took nerve for Susan Livingston to face that British raiding party and even more nerve to deceive them, but at no point did Susan have to fear for her safety. This was not the case a year later when six thousand British and German soldiers invaded New Jersey on the night of June 6, 1780. Once more the Livingstons were awakened by a midnight knock on their front door. This time the caller was an American, Brigadier General William Maxwell, commander of New Jersey's Continental Army Brigade. Grimly, he informed the Livingston women—the Governor as usual was in Trenton—that a formidable British army was landing at Elizabethtown. Its advance guard was already on the march. There was no hope of making a stand. Maxwell had only five hundred men. He was planning to retreat until the militia could turn out and reinforce him. He urged Mrs. Livingston and her daughters to come with him.

There was no need for discussion. The three women were in complete agreement. Their answer was a firm no. They were not going to abandon Liberty Hall to looting and burning. As the American General went off swearing into the night with his troops, Governor Livingston's family

settled down to await the arrival of the British at Liberty
Hall. Would it be the same Brigadier who had visited them
a year before? If so, he might feel that some revenge was in
order for Susan's treachery with her father's papers.

The night drained into dawn with no sign of the
British. By a marvelous stroke of luck, Brigadier Stirling
had met with an unfortunate accident while advancing
toward Liberty Hall. An American patrol had collided with
his column and blasted a single round at him. A bullet
smashed the Brigadier's thigh and sent him to the rear.

When the British column emerged from Elizabethtown, the man in charge was a German officer, Colonel Lud-
wig Johann Adolf von Wurmb, a handsome young daredevil
with quite a reputation as a lady killer. As the column
reached the gate of Liberty Hall, Susan Livingston stepped
onto the porch. Von Wurmb, who knew her by reputation,
immediately cantered up the path to get a better look at
one of the Three Graces. Doffing his hat, he introduced
himself.

Susan nodded and went straight to the point. "Are
you going to burn our house?"

The Colonel vowed that he had no such plan. When
Susan looked skeptical, he offered to prove his good inten-
tions by stationing sentries at Liberty Hall's gate to make
sure no straggler molested the mansion.

Instantly, Susan was all smiles. She pointed to a
trellis of bright red roses beside the porch and invited the
Colonel to pluck one as a token of her appreciation. The
Colonel did so, stuck the rose in his hat, and reiterated his
assurances that the Livingstons had no need to fear for
Liberty Hall. He also assured Susan that he and his troops
were planning to stay in New Jersey for a long time. Perhaps he could have the pleasure of calling on her?

Susan suspected that the citizens of New Jersey might

have some surprising ideas on that point, but she decided not to mention this to the Colonel. Instead, she thanked him for his courtesy and told him that whatever the outcome of the battle into which he was marching, she hoped that her rose would protect him from the bullets.

Off rode Colonel von Wurmb to find out that Miss Livingston's suspicions had been correct. The citizens of New Jersey, ably led by her father's good friend "Scotch Willie" Maxwell, soon demonstrated that they did not welcome the thought of becoming British subjects again.

Throughout a long, hot day, the German Colonel and his men, reinforced by the rest of the six-thousand-man British army, found their invasion route blocked by the hard fighting regulars of the New Jersey brigade, supported by swarms of militia. Late in the afternoon, George Washington appeared in the Short Hills with the main American army from Morristown, and all hope of a decisive victory vanished.

In a drenching rainstorm, pursued by violent thunder and lightning, the soggy, dispirited British and Germans retreated back to Elizabethtown. In the watery confusion, the sentries posted by Colonel von Wurmb at Liberty Hall vanished. A few minutes after the rear guard of the army passed the house, some of the flotsam and jetsam of war appeared. Most of them were stragglers drunk on the rum they had liberated from taverns and houses along the line of march. There were also a few disgruntled New Jersey Loyalists who had accompanied the royal army from New York, hoping for a victory that would restore them in triumph to their houses and farms.

This motley gang, ten or fifteen strong, surged up Liberty Hall's tree-lined drive and pounded on the door. When the Livingstons declined to open it, they smashed it in with the butts of their muskets. Susan, her mother, and her sister Kitty retreated to an upstairs bedroom. The servants locked themselves in the basement, but the intruders dragged them out and forced them to reveal that the Livingstons were upstairs. Outside, the storm mounted in fury, with thunder crashing and lightning racing down the sky.

One of the drunkest in the crowd drew a sword and announced that he would visit the ladies upstairs. Shuddering behind a bedroom door, Susan and her mother and sister could hear the clump of his heavy boots as he lurched up the two flights to the second floor.

It wasn't hard to imagine what would happen next. First, a roar of triumph at discovering the three helpless women. Then, the clatter of boots on the stairs as the rest of the drunken crew came rushing up to gloat over their spoils. Inflamed by alcohol and embittered by defeat, the men would most certainly resort to rape. After that, the women would be turned out of the house and their beloved Liberty Hall pillaged, plundered, and burned to the ground.

Everything Susan Livingston held dear was being threatened by these lawless intruders. Another woman, or even a man, might have decided the situation was hopeless and surrendered to despair. But beneath her flirtatious manner and fondness for fancy gowns Susan was a fighter. Like most fighters, she was motivated by two things—stubbornness and pride. Fortunately, both were tempered by a healthy dose of common sense.

Unarmed and outnumbered, Susan was in no position to defend herself by force. On the other hand, a shrewd assessment of the situation convinced her that timidity would only end in disaster. Determined to try to save herself, her family, and their home, Susan Livingston opted for that special brand of courage—boldness.

As the straggler reached the second-floor landing, Susan threw open the bedroom door and stepped out to confront him. Grabbing him by the collar, she spun the man around and threw him flat on his back. His sword went clattering down the stairs. At that precise moment, a tremendous crash of thunder shook the house and a bolt of lightning illuminated the countryside. The drunk, staring up at the unexpected apparition in a white dress, decided he was seeing a ghost, and with a squawk of terror, went flapping downstairs to rejoin his friend.

Instead of darting back to her refuge in the bedroom, Susan lit a candle and followed him. She marched down the stairs and confronted the unruly gang in the wide center hall. There was no coquetry in her manner now. She was all fire and ice.

She called them cowards, barbarians, criminals. She told them that Colonel von Wurmb, the commander of the advance guard, had assured her that Liberty Hall would not be touched. If they damaged any other part of the house or stole as much as a silver spoon, she swore that she would go straight to Colonel von Wurmb and demand that they be hanged. All of them!

Amazingly, the roughnecks submitted to this tongue-lashing from an unarmed woman. They stood there meek and silent. It was a marvelous demonstration of how courage can transform a situation. But how long would it last? By the light of her candle, Susan spied a familiar face in the crowd, a man she had known in less troubled days, now a Loyalist. Only a few months before, Susan had persuaded General Washington to permit the man's wife, another old friend, to visit her husband in New York. "I cannot believe that you are part of this crew of cutthroats," Susan said. "You have been a guest in this house. In spite of the fact that fate has put us on opposite sides of this terrible war, I *thought* we were still friends."

The shamefaced Loyalist collapsed completely. He tried to explain his presence by saying that he had only been looking for shelter from the rain.

Susan acidly informed him that he was free to use the barn, but she and her mother reserved the right to choose their own guests for their drawing room. "And they usually wipe off their boots before they come in," she added.

The chastened Loyalist decided it was time to join the British retreat. Taking charge of his cowed companions, he marched them out the door into the wind and rain.

No one molested Liberty Hall for the rest of the war. The word must have passed through the British ranks that a woman of courage lived there.

First Lady Under Fire

Although American women have never been officially involved in combat, a surprising number of them have distinguished themselves in wartime. Deborah Sampson Gannett disguised herself as a man, enlisted in the Continental Army and fought in several engagements before her true sex was discovered. Bridget Divers, wife of a Civil War private in the First Michigan Cavalry, often rode out with the men on scouting and raiding expeditions. Once, traveling with a wagon train that was attacked by Confederate cavalry, she took command of the poorly armed teamsters and fought off the rebel assault. Jacqueline Cochran ferried planes to the U. S. Eighth Air Force in England during World War II.

In one way or another, all of these women became part of a military unit. This fact certainly does not detract from their heroism. But I think most people will agree that the person who has the support of an organized group has a distinct advantage over the person who acts alone. Shared hardships foster a sense of pride and unity of purpose that can inspire even the most timid to perform superhuman feats.

For women, wartime service has always been a matter of choice. But in the days when our wars were fought on home ground, many American women who would never have gone out of their way to seek danger found themselves inadvertently drawn into its circle. I have always been impressed by how one of them, Dolley Madison, rose to the challenge.

This plump vivacious First Lady faced a personal as well as a national crisis—the burning of Washington by British troops during the War of 1812. Defying her husband's orders to flee to safety and acting entirely on her own—practically everyone else in the capital had long since vanished—Dolley provided the nation with a superb combination of leadership, patriotism, housewifely thrift, and feminine grace under pressure.

War clouds were already gathering on the national horizon when James Madison took his oath of office in 1809. As a side effect of England's battle against Napoleon, English warships claimed the right to stop and search American vessels on the high seas. In the course of these searches, British naval officers regularly pressed into His Majesty's service any American sailors they suspected of being Englishmen.

Napoleon took an equally high-handed attitude toward American shipping. He not only forbade the United States to trade with Great Britain but ordered his fleet to fire on any vessel that allowed itself to be boarded by British officers. Both countries' policies were detested in the United States.

Despite the efforts of Madison's predecessor, Thomas Jefferson, and of Madison himself, neither England nor France would halt their harassment of American ships.

Although the American people were united in their feelings of anger about the situation, their rage was channeled in two sharply different directions. Madison's party, the Jeffersonian Republicans (ancestors of today's Democrats), roundly condemned Great Britain but harbored little resentment against the French. Their opponents, the Federal-

LIBRARY OF CONGRESS

This rare photograph of Dolley Madison was taken on July 4, 1848. She died the following July at the age of 81.

THE BETTMANN ARCHIVE INC.

This print dramatizes Dolley's rescue of a copy of the Declaration of Independence and other White House documents as the British approached.

ists, on the other hand, were violently pro-British and just as violently anti-French. They were inclined to blame the whole problem on bungled negotiations by the Republicans, and the prime target of their fury soon became James Madison.

I know from experience that the barbs of the critics are more painful for a President's family to endure than they are for the President. Dolley must have been hurt by the mounting public hostility to her husband. But she had suffered public hostility in the past, and survived.

Dolley was the daughter of Virginia parents who moved to Philadelphia when she was fourteen. Perhaps in defiance of snobbish city folk, she persisted in spelling her name with an "e" because that was the way the clerk of the country parish had written it in the register when she was baptized. It was a small sign of her personal resistance to the life her parents had chosen for themselves and their family. A Quaker convert, Dolley's father practiced his faith with fervor. He joined the wing of the Quaker movement which banned all worldly show in clothes, jewelry, or household furnishings. Other Quakers (called "wet" because their principles were supposedly limp) were more inclined to enjoy life.

Dolley's normal, Virginia-bred high spirits were frowned on by the elders of her meeting as flirtations with Satan. She secretly defied them by wearing a brooch on her dress, concealed by a kerchief. But she did not dare attend the dances and plays that other girls her age enjoyed in booming Philadelphia. That might have brought her a public denunciation at the Sunday meeting.

Quakers made significant contributions to the tradition of feminine courage in America by treating men and women as equals and encouraging their members to oppose moral complacency and inhumanity wherever they saw it. But the version of the faith Dolley encountered apparently undid these positive influences by a fiercely negative approach to almost everything else.

The meeting's control of its members extended to the choice of a marriage partner. It was strictly forbidden to marry outside the faith. Here, too, Dolley showed signs of rebellion. She put off, delayed, evaded John Todd, a well-to-do Quaker lawyer, for over two years. Only the pleas of her father on his deathbed persuaded her to say yes.

Two years after Dolley's marriage, her younger sister Lucy eloped with George Steptoe Washington, a nephew of President Washington. She was promptly read out of the Quaker meeting—a grim experience similar to excommunication. Dolley heard her sister condemned for "the accomplishment of her marriage with a person not in membership with us, before a hireling priest." In spite of this fire-and-brimstone beginning, Lucy's marriage proved to be a happy one.

A year later, John Todd died in the yellow fever epidemic of 1793. His lively twenty-five-year-old widow was soon being wooed by a number of important politicians who were spending much of their time in Philadelphia, which was then the nation's capital. Among the suitors were Senator Aaron Burr of New York and Congressman James Madison of Virginia. Dolley was drawn to the shy, spare little Virginian in spite of the seventeen-year difference in their ages. Madison's twinkling blue eyes intimated—and his conversation soon confirmed—a sense of humor which he carefully concealed from the public. But he was not a Quaker, and it took all Dolley's courage to accept his offer of marriage. Years later, she revealed in a letter how "our Society used to control me entirely" and spoke of her "ancient terror of them." On her wedding night she wrote an emotional letter to a friend, lamenting her Philadelphia "enemies" who were smearing her reputation for marrying "the man who of all others I most admire."

It is never easy to break with a childhood faith and modify it according to one's adult understanding. When the decision is made by a woman as part of a personal commitment to a man, it becomes a form of courage. For Dolley, it intensified her dedication to her husband—and his devotion to her. But Dolley did not entirely turn her back on her Quaker past. She abandoned the austere prohibitions against stylish clothes and balls and parties but she retained the Quaker virtues of honesty and charity.

By charity I mean generosity of spirit. It was, I believe, the secret of Dolley's charisma. Long before anyone used this word, Dolley personified it. But to work for a lifetime, this kind of personal power has to be based on genuine feelings. When the feelings are false, the charisma very quickly disintegrates into mere charm. Dolley's charisma was rooted in her Quaker belief in the goodness of most people, even when they were behaving atrociously for political reasons. She also possessed several talents that any politician would envy—a gift for remembering names and faces, and a knack for saying the right thing at the right time.

Dolley's banquets, balls, and Wednesday "levees" were among the liveliest parties in Washington. Only the staunchest President-haters had the willpower to boycott them. Washington Irving, a diehard Federalist, attended one White House reception and came away charmed. He described the First Lady as "a fine, portly, buxom dame, who has a smile and a pleasant word for everybody." But even Dolley's delightful personality could not induce him to say a good word about her husband. The author dismissed the President as "a withered Apple-john."

Soon after the Madisons moved into the White House, Congress appropriated funds to decorate the mansion. The building had been little more than half finished when its first occupants, John and Abigail Adams, arrived in 1800.

The walls lacked plaster, temporary wooden steps stood at all the doors, and the now magnificent East Room was fit only for hanging the wash. The "President's Palace" was finally completed during Thomas Jefferson's second term. By the time Dolley Madison became First Lady, it was time to start worrying about its furnishings.

Dolley began decorating two rooms on the main floor —the Ladies' Drawing Room (the present Red Room) and the Oval Drawing Room (the present Blue Room). Working with architect Benjamin Latrobe, she selected furnishings in the "very latest Sheraton style."

The Ladies' Drawing Room was done in yellow, with high-backed sofas and chairs upholstered in bright yellow satin and a yellow damask fireboard in front of the mantel. The Oval Room was even more splendid. Latrobe and Dolley furnished it with a Brussels carpet, bronze lamps, and thirty-six specially designed Grecian chairs. The predominant color was red, and the long graceful windows, one of the most striking features of the room, were handsomely draped in crimson velvet.

Dolley used part of the congressional appropriation to purchase new silver and crystal and a set of blue and gold Lowestoft china for the State Dining Room. At Latrobe's suggestion, she hung a large gold-framed portrait of George Washington on the main wall. The painting had been started by Gilbert Stuart and completed by a later painter named Winstanley.

Dolley Madison's interior decorating came to a halt in 1811. She had already spent about $12,000 on the mansion, and there was no hope of getting additional funds because the nation was by now perilously close to war. The congressional elections of 1810 had brought a new coalition of young Republicans to power. Predominantly southerners and westerners, they were more fervently anti-British than the rest of their party—mainly because they and their constituents hoped to make a quick fortune in real estate from British-held Canada and West Florida.

Under the leadership of Henry Clay of Kentucky and John C. Calhoun of South Carolina, the War Hawks began pushing for a showdown with the British over the impressment of American seamen. The congressional vote was extremely close—79 to 49 in the House and 19 to 13 in the Senate—but the War Hawks prevailed. On June 19, 1812, President Madison signed a declaration of war against Great Britain.

The first year of the conflict brought a series of shattering American defeats. The Federalists were livid. "Mr. Madison's War" was denounced in highly inflammatory terms. Worse, there was a woeful decline of public confidence in the presidency. New England, a Federalist stronghold, was in a virtual state of secession. In Vermont, the Governor ordered the state militia to resign from national service. In Massachusetts there was talk of negotiating a separate peace with the enemy.

"That little man in the palace," his enemies called the five-foot-six-inch Madison, who was savagely roasted in Federalist newspapers. "The white house" became a term of opprobrium and was regularly spelled with small letters to indicate disapproval of its occupant.

The Madisons' private life became the subject of venomous rumors and gossip. Dolley was criticized for using snuff in public and was suspected of wearing rouge. She was also accused of being unfaithful to her husband; he in turn was whispered to be impotent.

A Federalist clergyman, the Reverend Mr. Breckinridge, tongue-lashed Dolley when she showed up in his congregation one Sunday. His chief complaint was that she had given dinner parties on the Sabbath, but he was also incensed at Congress, which had recently passed a law allowing the mail to be moved on Sunday. The minister insisted that vengeance would be exacted for these sins.

"It is the government that will be punished," he roared, "and, as with Nineveh of old, it will not be the habitations of the people, but your temples and your palaces that will be burned to the ground."

Even the Reverend Mr. Breckinridge must have been stunned when, not long after his sermon, his dire prediction came true.

In the fall of 1813, it became apparent that the British intended to strike a blow at the nation's capital. Their ships moved freely up and down Chesapeake Bay, and British officers in disguise visited Washington with impunity. The Admiral in command of the fleet, George Cockburn, boldly announced that he would soon make his bow in Mrs. Madison's drawing room. But for the better part of a year, the British did not attack. They waged a war of nerves, obviously hoping that the mere threat of an assault might incite the local citizens against the President.

The Washington state of mind was ample justification for such a shrewd policy. Even then, in its infancy, the capital was an emotional, gossip-ridden city, and the distraught citizens were soon taking out their tensions on President Madison. The slanders against him became more and more vicious, and there were rumors of an assassination plot, which would make a British invasion superfluous.

When worried friends urged Dolley to leave the city, she came close to losing her temper for perhaps the first time in her life. "I am determined to stay with my husband," she said. She began sleeping with a Tunisian saber, a souvenir of the war with the Barbary pirates, beside her bed. The President revealed some steel of his own beneath his shy, introverted personality. He ordered a troop of militia stationed on the White House grounds. Panic-prone Washington got the Madison message. No one was running the President of the United States out of the White House without a fight.

On August 19, 1814, the British finally decided to strike. A fleet carrying a raiding force of 4,500 veteran infantrymen dropped anchor at the mouth of the Patuxent River in Maryland, less than a day's march from Washington. Madison's Secretary of War, John Armstrong, insisted that they had no intention of attacking the capital and refused to enforce the President's orders to defend the city. Only when the British debarked at Benedict, Maryland, a few days later, and began marching toward the capital, did Armstrong frantically start collecting the various regiments and brigades which he had scattered up and down the coastline.

By then it was too late. The six thousand amateur militiamen and the few hundred sailors and marines Armstrong assembled were an army in name only. They had neither discipline, organization, nor esprit de corps. With the British attack a virtual certainty, President Madison decided to ride out to the battlefield. There was a chance that his presence might give the untrained soldiers an extra measure of confidence.

The President expected to be gone only overnight, but he hesitated to leave Dolley behind in the White House. A timid woman would have retreated to safer quarters in Virginia. But Dolley cheerfully assured her harassed husband that she was not in the least afraid to stay in the White House without him, no matter what everyone else in Washington decided to do. I have the feeling that she was trying to encourage the President, who was anything but sure of himself on military matters.

The following day, August 23, Madison sent Dolley a report that the American troops were in good spirits, and

he was optimistic that they could hold off the British invaders. Before the day was over, however, the President was
forced to change his mind. Two British deserters had been
brought before him, and he asked the enemy soldiers if the
British army was as strong as the American force they could
see all around them. With a grim smile, the two redcoats
replied, "We think it is."

Soon a report of what the British soldiers had told the
President was circulating throughout Washington, creating
instant panic. A mass exodus began. Horses and wagons became as scarce as competent generals. Dolley watched the
frantic excitement from the White House but remained un-
touched by it. She had seen a similar panic in the yellow
fever epidemic of 1793, which had turned Philadelphia into
a ghost town. Perhaps she remembered that Quakers were
among the few who stayed to nurse the writhing victims of
that plague. Perhaps simply surviving one panic is the best
recipe for dealing with the next one. At any rate, Dolley
stood her ground.

Then came word from her husband which made her
wonder if even the President was succumbing to the general
fright. He told her to be ready to leave the White House at
a moment's notice and begged her to make sure his presidential papers were not left behind.

Even in 1814, when Presidents did not accumulate
enough papers to fill a library, this was no small order. Mr.
Madison had been in office five years. Dolley instantly summoned the White House chief steward, Jean Pierre Sioussat.
Called French John, he had been Thomas Jefferson's door-
man. Dolley had promoted him to his present post. She told
him to find a horse and carriage, even if he had to beg,
borrow, or steal them. French John proved Dolley was a
good judge of character. Resourcefulness, the ability to deal
with the unexpected, is a must in a White House steward.

He was back within the hour with a horse and wagon. Dolley did not ask him where he got them. She personally packed the President's papers into a big leatherbound trunk and ordered them to be taken immediately to a hiding place in the country.

I shudder to think of what the British could have done with those papers if they had captured them. They would have used selective quotations from them to make the President look like a crook, a fool, a coward, a liar—just about anything that would help to drive him from office. Once they accomplished that feat, America might have been theirs for dismembering.

With her husband's papers safe, there was no vital reason for Dolley to remain in the White House. But she stayed anyway. She was hoping her presence would persuade some Washingtonians to ignore the pervasive panic and organize a defense of the city. Like most First Ladies, she felt an intense personal responsibility for the mansion. She encouraged the servants by telling them that the President would return at any moment with good news from the battlefield. Then they would have the laugh on all those brave residents of the capital who were running for Virginia.

Alas, on the battlefield, Madison's worst military fears were coming true. Secretary of War Armstrong still kept saying that the British had no intention of marching on Washington. He did allow Captain Joshua Barney to place a battery of guns across the road to the capital. But Barney and his sailors received no support from the ragtag army Armstrong had assembled. The battle of Bladensburg was little more than a skirmish. After a few rounds, the militia broke and galloped for the horizon. All hope of defending Washington vanished with them.

On the morning of the battle of Bladensburg, August 24, Dolley was up at dawn. She stationed herself on the

White House roof, spyglass in hand, hoping to catch sight of her husband in the distance. But there was no sign of the President. All she saw were swarms of people and wagons piled high with trunks and household goods streaming steadily toward the bridge that led across the Potomac to Virginia.

As the morning wore on, Dolley could hear the boom of cannons echoing in the distance. It soon became obvious that the battle was turning into a rout. Groups of frightened and dispirited militiamen began straggling into the city. Many of them had turned tail and run when a new British weapon, low-flying Congreve rockets, came tearing into their ranks.

As the news of the American defeat and the imminent British arrival spread through the capital, the rush to escape became even more frantic. The militia assigned to protect the White House deserted their posts and disappeared among the masses of people hurrying toward the Potomac.

Still Dolley refused to budge. She ordered the servants to prepare dinner for the President and his Cabinet and told them to set out some wine on the sideboard in the dining room. By now, she must have been seriously worried about her husband's safety, but the orders helped steady the morale of the White House staff and kept them from joining the general flight from the city. She was demonstrating better leadership in the crisis than any American male, including her husband, showed on this dismal day.

The preparations for dinner were well underway when a pair of horsemen covered with dust appeared at the White House door. They brought a message from President Madison urging Dolley to leave Washington at once. But Dolley was still loath to abandon the White House. If she only had a cannon to station at every window, she vowed that she would stay and defend the mansion herself. French

John had a better idea. He suggested a gunpowder booby trap that would blow up the British if they opened the front gate.

Dolley vetoed this plan. Her cool head now conceded the necessity of retreating from the White House. But she still declined to panic. She would take as much as she could carry with her. French John was ordered to find another horse and carriage, which he promptly did. If there had been an Avis-Rent-A-Horse around in 1814, he would have been a natural to run it. He certainly believed in trying harder. Dolley ordered the crimson draperies in the Oval Room taken down and packed into John's latest vehicle. Next came some valuable books and the White House silverware. Then Dolley's eyes fell on the portrait of George Washington in the State Dining Room. She was appalled by the thought of leaving the father of the country to the mercy of the enemies he had once defeated. God knows what they might do to it— set it up on the White House lawn and use it for target practice perhaps. The British sense of humor was peculiar.

With the coolness of a soldier determined to retreat with honor, Dolley pointed to the portrait. "Take it down," she said.

French John rushed to comply. The massive gilt frame had been screwed to the wall. French John put two men to work removing it, but the screws were driven so deeply into the plaster that it would take hours to get them out. An old friend of the Madisons, Mr. Carroll, arrived at the White House while the two men were toiling away. He had come to escort Dolley to safety, and he was not very happy when she insisted on waiting until the picture was removed.

Mr. Carroll fretted and fidgeted, and Dolley finally ordered the men to abandon their screwdrivers and break the frame. The canvas was carefully removed and sent off with two trusted messengers to a farmhouse in Virginia. The last thing Dolley swooped up was a framed copy of the Declaration of Independence. Then she ordered French John to lock the front door and deliver her pet parrot to the home of the French minister for safekeeping.

Mr. Carroll was still snorting impatiently when Jim Smith, President Madison's black servant, came galloping up to the front door shouting, "Clear out! Clear out!" This time Dolley obeyed. She put on her bonnet, stepped into her carriage, and set off for the home of a friend in Rokeby, Virginia, a mile away.

The British, led by Admiral Cockburn and Major General Robert Ross, entered Washington that night. They set fire to the Capitol and then marched down Pennsylvania Avenue to the White House. Smashing the locks on the front door, they burst into the deserted mansion around eight o'clock.

The spits of meat were still sizzling over the coals; the wine, in handsome glass decanters, was sitting on the sideboard. Admiral Cockburn poured a glass for himself and his officers and drank a mocking toast to President Madison's health. Then, after taking a yellow cushion from the Ladies' Drawing Room as a souvenir, he ordered his troops to pile all the furnishings in the middle of the East Room and set them on fire. By eleven o'clock, the mansion was a huge, blazing pyre. Similar fires burned at the Navy Yard, the Treasury, and other public buildings.

The next day Dolley journeyed on to Wiley's Tavern, near Little Falls, Virginia, where she and her husband were finally reunited. The President arrived about noon and stayed with Dolley until midnight. He then set out to rejoin the American army, which had regrouped and was now marching to defend Baltimore, the next British target.

Dolley refused to remain a refugee in Virginia. As soon as Madison sent word that the British had left Washington, she returned to the charred and ruined city. Her beloved White House was a burnt-out shell. Heartbroken at the sight, Dolley wrote to the wife of Benjamin Latrobe, "I cannot tell you what I felt."

Like most courageous people, Dolley Madison had acted out of an inner sense of what was right. She had no way of knowing that her dramatic rescue of George Washington's portrait would silence her husband's critics and infuse the once-divided nation with a new spirit. The day after the news of the British burning of the White House reached New York, huge numbers of volunteers, including many women, rushed to complete the construction of Fort Greene in Brooklyn. In Baltimore, a local orator declared, "The spirit of the nation is aroused." The furious defense of that city by the men manning Fort McHenry made the British think twice about further forays ashore. The battle prompted one former opponent of "Mr. Madison's War" to change his mind rather dramatically. Inspired by the American flag defiantly waving in the midst of the rockets' red glare, Francis Scott Key wrote our national anthem.

Key was not the only defector from the Federalist ranks. All along the Atlantic seaboard, people who had been denouncing the war and talking surrender abruptly changed their minds. In less than a month came news of a shattering American victory over the British invasion fleet on Lake Champlain. Confronted by a united, determined people, the British were more than willing to sign a peace treaty six months later.

With the White House uninhabitable, the Madisons moved into nearby Octagon House. (Why it was given this name is a mystery, since it is partly triangular and partly circular in shape.) In this elegant brick mansion Dolley soon resumed her popular Wednesday evening receptions. Now she was everyone's favorite. Criticism dwindled to the vanishing point—and so did the President's political opposition. For talking treason and secession, the Federalist party practically went out of business—and President Madison's successor, James Monroe, ushered in eight years of what came to be called "the era of good feeling." I like to believe that a lot of these good feelings flowered from the genius—and above all, the courage—of Dolley Madison.

Ordeal in the Owyhee Country

As anyone who has ever seen a cowboy movie knows, two basic ingredients of courage in a crisis are daring and physical prowess. How often have we watched western heroes from William S. Hart to John Wayne display their nerve and muscles in exclusively male duels to the death. In the mythical old West, men were men and women were hardly visible. But in the real West, a woman once displayed more daring and endurance than all the males in sight.

Sarah Winnemucca's Indian name was Thocmetony or Shell Flower. She belonged to a tribe called the Southern Paiutes who lived in what is now the state of Nevada. I don't know which tribe suffered more injustices at the hands of the white men but I would venture to guess that the Southern Paiutes must be near the top of the list. The most tragic part of their long agony is that they were a docile, peace-loving people who wanted nothing more than to work their farms and live in harmony with their neighbors.

The Southern Paiutes had their first contact with white men in the early 1840s when small groups of traders and explorers began trickling into Nevada and setting up outposts on Paiute lands. Sarah, who was only a child at the time, was petrified of the newcomers with their noisy guns and pale skins, but the rest of the Southern Paiutes welcomed the white settlers.

The friendship was cemented when, in the winter of 1845, Sarah's grandfather, Chief Winnemucca, accompanied Captain John Fremont on an expedition across the Sierra Nevada Mountains to California. Winnemucca returned full of admiration for the white man's ways. Unfortunately, by the time he died in 1860, the spirit of trust and goodwill that had existed between the two peoples was beginning to disintegrate.

Another tribe of Nevada Indians, who were more warlike than the Southern Paiutes, had become involved in several skirmishes with the white settlers. After one particularly bloody encounter, the whites herded all the Indians in the region onto the Pyramid Lake Reservation in northern Nevada.

The Southern Paiutes were told that the move would be to their advantage. They would be given larger and more productive farms, and the government would supply them with food and clothing. As it turned out, the Indian agent who ran the reservation had little interest in his charges' welfare. He cheated them out of their rations and spent most of his time scheming to line his own pockets at their expense. Sarah Winnemucca was the only member of her tribe who was not shocked at the white man's duplicity.

Sarah had lost her childhood fear of whites after she became ill with a mysterious fever and a white woman nursed her back to health. Later, as a teenager, she had lived with the family of a white stage-company agent and served as a companion to his daughter. By then, Sarah had forgotten her earlier antipathy to whites. She learned to speak English, dropped her Indian name of Thocmetony, and assumed the Christian name Sarah.

NEVADA HISTORICAL SOCIETY

This is my favorite picture of Sarah Winnemucca. Doesn't she look like the daughter of a chief?

Chief Winnemucca was so pleased to see his grand-daughter adopting the ways of his friends, the whites, that he decreed on his deathbed that she continue her education at St. Mary's Convent School in San Jose, California. The sixteen-year-old had barely arrived when the parents of the white students began complaining about sending their daughters to school with an Indian girl. Three weeks later, Sarah Winnemucca was on her way back to Nevada. Her early distrust of whites had returned, but this time it was more than a childhood phobia; she had good reason to view them with a wary eye.

Sarah's father, Winnemucca II, was now chief of the Southern Paiutes. Not knowing how to deal with the unscrupulous Indian agent at Pyramid Lake, the chief and his tribe had solved the problem by wandering away from the reservation and attaching themselves to a nearby army post. Contrary to the usual image of the U. S. Cavalry as bloodthirsty Indian haters, the soldiers treated the Paiutes kindly, sharing their rations and finding odd jobs for them at the post. Sarah, who had a natural gift for languages, became an interpreter. She knew three different Indian tongues and had mastered Spanish as well as English.

In 1875, the Southern Paiutes were finally given an official home. The government moved them to a vast tract of land in southeast Oregon called Malheur Reservation. The soil was good, the climate pleasant, and although they were still under the supervision of the government, their new agent, Samuel Parrish, was that rarity in the Indian Bureau, an honest and sympathetic man. He saw to it that his charges were well supplied with food and clothing, assigned them individual grain fields, and allowed them to keep the crops they raised. Under Parrish's supervision, the Paiutes worked hard and took pride in their farms. It was a bitter blow to them when Parrish was abruptly removed and a new agent, William V. Rinehart, appointed in his place.

Like most Indian agents, Rinehart had obtained his position through political influence and had no interest in the Indians or their problems. He abolished the individual farms, made all the Indians work for him and, instead of wages, paid them for their labor with the food and clothing that were supposed to be given to them as gifts from the government.

Several other Indian tribes also lived at Malheur. One of them, the Northern Paiutes, expressed their contempt for William Rinehart by walking off the reservation and joining forces with the Bannock Indians in neighboring Idaho, who were preparing to go on the warpath.

The Southern Paiutes took a less aggressive approach to their problems. Since Sarah Winnemucca knew the white man's tongue, they asked her to be their spokesman. She went to the nearest army camp and asked the commanding officer to appeal to the federal government on behalf of her people for the dismissal of Rinehart and the reappointment of Samuel Parrish. The government ignored the request and worse yet, informed William Rinehart that Sarah Winnemucca had organized a plot against him. The infuriated agent vowed to be even tougher with the Paiutes and began by banishing Sarah from Malheur.

A few weeks later, in June of 1878, the Bannock uprising began. Sarah had gone to live with some of her tribesmen in the John Day Valley not far from the reservation. She learned about the uprising only by accident. She had been hired to drive two white men and one of their daughters from Oregon to Silver City, Idaho. Sarah had taken the wagon trail to Silver City many times before. There were a number of settlements along the way where travelers stopped to rest and exchange news with the inhabitants. On this trip, however, the settlements were deserted. There were no men working in the fields, no women hanging out washing, no children playing in the yard.

The four travelers heard the clopping of horses' hooves in the distance. A detachment of cavalry came galloping up the road. Their commanding officer gravely informed Sarah and her passengers that they were traveling at the risk of their lives. The Bannock Indians were on the warpath. All the white settlers in the region had taken refuge at Fort Lyon, a few miles away. The soldiers urged the travelers to do the same.

At the army post, Sarah learned more about the Bannock uprising. It had started with an attack on some white families on Big Camas Prairie a few days before. Next, the Bannocks captured a stagecoach bringing military supplies to the fort. They seized two boxes of Winchester rifles and hundreds of rounds of ammunition.

Sarah was not surprised to learn that the Northern Paiutes, who had left Malheur Reservation in rebellion against William Rinehart, had become the Bannocks' allies in their war against the whites. She was horrified at the next piece of news. A raiding party of Northern Paiutes had swooped down on Malheur, kidnapped a large band of Southern Paiutes, including Sarah's father and brother, and forced them to join the Bannock camp.

Sarah was not the only one who was upset at this news. The commanding officer at Fort Lyon, the former Civil War hero General O. O. Howard, had been trying for days to contact Chief Winnemucca II. He wanted to let him know that the army was aware that he and his people were unwilling captives and to tell him that if they could escape from the Bannocks and reach Fort Lyon, the soldiers would see that they were well treated.

General Howard tried to find someone to take his message to the Southern Paiutes. The scouts and trappers who were usually available for such missions refused. The Bannocks had taken their prisoners to a hiding place high in the mountains of present-day Owyhee County, Idaho, over a hundred miles away. Whoever made the trip would have to contend with some of the most forbidding terrain in America, a landscape of black basalt bluffs towering against pale washes, where even sagebrush and greasewood grow precariously. If a messenger reached the Bannock encampment, how would he get his message to Chief Winnemucca? The Bannocks were sure to have sharp-eyed warriors continuously studying the barren landscape. Any outsider would be killed on sight.

Aside from the problem of finding the Bannock camp, General Howard was loath to attack it while the friendly Southern Paiutes were captives. They might be the worst sufferers in a pitched battle. He asked Sarah if she would volunteer to carry his message of peace and refuge to her father.

Howard was asking a thirty-four-year-old woman to undertake a journey that had already scared off a half dozen rugged frontiersmen. A thirty-four-year-old Indian woman who had experienced the cruel prejudice that infected the minds of too many white Americans. It is not hard to imagine the welter of conflicting emotions that must have assailed Sarah Winnemucca. A white man was asking her to undertake this suicide mission. If she agreed, there was a very good chance that she would die of starvation wandering through the unmapped desolate lava wastes of the Owyhee country. If she refused, she might have to live with the knowledge that her father, her brother, and several dozen members of her tribe had died because she did not try to save them.

In the beginning, a voice deep inside Sarah Winnemucca must have snarled a silent NO to General Howard's request. There were plenty of reasons to suspect the offer, beyond her already strong distrust of white men. What if the General was only using her to start a civil war between her father's people and the Bannocks? If the Indians started killing each other, it would be that much easier for the cavalry to finish them off.

But Oliver O. Howard was no ordinary general. A gentle, deeply religious man, he had been a leading supporter of bringing black Americans into the Union army during the Civil War and keeping them there after the war. For him, the great conflict had been a crusade against slavery. He had paid a price for his commitment; one sleeve of his uniform was empty. Without making speeches, Howard communicated his passionate belief in human equality, regardless of skin color, to Sarah Winnemucca. Supporting this fragile trust was the profound tribal loyalty that was part of Sarah's Indian heritage. Most whites find it hard to understand this feeling of community. To Sarah Winnemucca, daughter and granddaughter of chiefs, it was as natural as breathing. Woven through her childhood were memories of tribal celebrations in which women played prominent roles. Her favorite was the Festival of Flowers, when the young girls gathered blossoms and wove them into garlands. "Come and be happy with me," they had sung. "I shall be beautiful while the earth lasts. Dance and be happy with me."

In the name of this lost happiness and her heritage as the daughter of a chief, Sarah Winnemucca accepted the responsibility the white General asked her to take. On a horse supplied by Howard, she set out for the Bannock camp with two Indian scouts, John and George Paiute, as guides. They rode along the banks of the Owyhee River for about fifteen miles until they came to the remains of a Bannock campsite. There were clumps of hair on the ground, and strings of beads had been broken and scattered around—part of the Bannock mourning ritual for a slain chief.

"The Bannocks' chief, Buffalo Horn, must have been killed in the fighting," Sarah said with a shudder. There was no need to add that the trip would be even more perilous now because the Bannocks would be eager to avenge his death.

A few miles farther along, Sarah and her companions stopped to rest at a deserted farmhouse. Everything flammable, furniture, bedding, and clothes, had been hauled out of the house, piled in the yard, and burned. The fire was still smoldering when they rode up, and there were fresh footprints in the soil. The Bannocks had obviously left only a short time before.

Soon after, the travelers came to a fork in the road. One of the paths was a newly blazed trail that led straight into the mountains. They took it and, a few miles later, came across further ominous evidence that they were on the right track. On the side of the road, they found a stage driver's whip, a clock, and a fiddle. Sarah had no doubts that the owners of all three items were no longer alive to claim them.

The trail grew steeper and more treacherous. Several times, Sarah was almost pitched out of the saddle when her horse lost his footing on the bare stone. Washington Irving, on a trip West, had visited this part of Idaho and described it as "a vast uninhabited solitude, with precipitous cliffs and yawning ravines, looking like the ruins of a world." The trail wound along huge granite scarps and ledges over one-thousand-foot gorges cut by creeks whose waters barely saw the sun. It was a desert, not of sand, but of rock, uninhabited by man. The sun beat down on the riders, as pitiless as the landscape through which they toiled.

Suddenly Sarah's guides reined in their horses. They pointed to two figures on the slope of a mountain in the distance. They were definitely Indians, but from the distance it was hard to tell whether they were Bannocks or Paiutes. Gambling on the hope that they were fellow tribesmen, Sarah called and waved her handkerchief. As they drew closer, she was relieved to see that not only were they Paiutes but one of them was her brother Lee.

Although Lee was happy to see Sarah, he had only bad news to give her. "Our people are all prisoners of the Bannocks," he reported mournfully. "They have been stripped of their weapons; their horses and blankets have been taken, and they have been very badly treated."

When Sarah told Lee that she had come to bring a message to their father, he could only shake his head. "The Bannocks will kill you," he warned. "They have threatened to kill everyone who comes with messages from the white people. Indians who bring messages are enemies, they say. They tell us this all the time and threaten us with terrible tortures if we side with the white men."

Sarah shrugged off her brother's warning. She had come this far and she was determined not to stop until she had seen her father.

For the first part of the journey, Sarah had been dressed in her usual white woman's clothes. Now she took an Indian blanket out of her saddlebag and began dabbing paint on her face. By the time she was finished, she looked like an authentic squaw.

Lee Winnemucca told his sister that the Bannock encampment was just beyond the next mountain. Knowing the positions of the Bannock lookouts, he told Sarah how to circle the camp and approach it from the north, where the terrain was so rough the Bannocks thought lookouts were unnecessary. Sarah tied her horse to a tree, said good-bye to her brother and her two guides, and started up the trail on foot. It was an agonizing journey. The granite and basalt slopes were so steep that she often had to crawl along on her hands and knees. Knifelike edges of rock cut her palms and fingers and tore at her legs as she struggled across the gouged, eroded slopes. Finally, she found herself on a tree-covered hillside above a mountain lake, looking down on the Bannock camp. It was big. Sarah counted over three hundred lodges and close to a thousand warriors.

Hiding in the trees until nightfall, Sarah crept down the hillside into the camp. She quickly located the lodges where the Paiutes were being held. First she pretended to be fussing over some animal skins that had been hung up to dry, then she picked up a load of kindling wood and slipped into her father's lodge. Her paint and blanket confused the Paiutes. It took them a few minutes to realize who she was. As soon as they recognized her, they whispered excitedly, "Oh, Sarah, you've come to save us!"

"Perhaps," Sarah said. "First I must talk to my father."

Chief Winnemucca and his daughter sat down in one corner of the lodge to discuss General Howard's message. At first the Chief was reluctant to leave the Bannock camp. "If we are caught," he said, "we will all be killed."

"If you stay here," Sarah reminded him, "the Bannocks will force you to fight with them."

Chief Winnemucca shook his head emphatically, "My people do not want war."

"But if you don't fight, the Bannocks will slaughter you," Sarah said.

Sarah talked with her father for a long time. Several times during their discussion, Bannock guards came in to check on their prisoners.

In her squaw's costume, Sarah looked just like the other Paiute women, so the Bannocks never realized there was an intruder in their camp. Nor, since they did not understand the Paiute language, could they know what a crucial decision was being made.

Sarah finally convinced Chief Winnemucca that escape was his only choice. "Trust in me," she promised, "I will lead you to safety."

Stealing out of her father's lodge, Sarah made her way down the line of Paiute lodges and hastily whispered instructions to the captives inside. One by one, under cover of the darkness, they crept out of the camp. Seventy-five Paiutes, including Chief Winnemucca, fled along the trail the Bannocks had blazed through the mountains. Around midnight, they were joined by Lee Winnemucca and John and George Paiute, Sarah's guides. They brought with them horses that they had taken from the Bannock herd. The Bannocks had originally stolen them from the Paiutes.

Sarah took charge of the advance party, while her brother Lee and some twenty Paiute braves formed a rear guard. At Sarah's insistence, the fugitives traveled all night. At dawn, after six hours on the trail, they reached a settlement called Summit Springs. Sarah decided it was safe to stop and rest. The Paiutes had barely dismounted when one of Lee Winnemucca's scouts came galloping up to them. "We are followed by the Bannocks!" he cried. "They've fired at our rear guard and they're heading this way."

Remounting their horses, the exhausted Paiutes took off again. If the Bannocks caught up to them, they would never reach Fort Lyon alive. Sarah decided to ride ahead and sound the alarm. Taking her sister-in-law Mattie and John and George Paiute, she set off at a gallop for the army outpost at Sheep Ranch.

General Howard was already at the outpost, anxiously awaiting Sarah's return. It was about 5:30 in the afternoon of June 14. General Howard was in the office of the former stage station when a sentry shouted, "There's a mounted party in sight!"

A few minutes later, Sarah Winnemucca came galloping into Sheep Ranch, leaped from her horse, and burst into tears. She had ridden 223 miles in three days and two nights, with no sleep and very little to eat or drink. It took Sarah several minutes to regain her composure. When she was finally able to speak, she told General Howard that her father and the other Paiutes were about twenty miles away. She asked him to send a detachment of soldiers to bring them safely back to Fort Lyon.

General Howard went into action, revealing under his gentle manner the toughness and efficiency of the professional soldier. Orders were shouted to the waiting troopers. Bugles blared. Within minutes the cavalry was racing to the rescue of Sarah's father and brother and the rest of the Southern Paiutes. It would have confused John Wayne fans to see those blue-coated troopers thundering down the road to save not a white wagon train but a tribe of Indians in danger of getting killed by other Indians. History is a lot more complicated than Hollywood's version of it.

Once her tribespeople were safe, Sarah gave General Howard a detailed report of the Bannock encampment. She told him how many warriors there were, how many horses they had, the exact location of their camp, and the best way to get to it. Howard soon mounted an expedition against the Bannocks, and the uprising was quelled. Except for one brief flurry of fighting the following year, it was the end of warfare between white men and red men in Idaho.

I wish I could tell you that Sarah Winnemucca and her tribe lived happily ever after. Unfortunately, they did not—but that's another story. I can tell you, however, that through all the Paiutes' subsequent tribulations, Sarah's courage never wavered. She remained their principal champion, and after a six-year struggle, persuaded the United States Senate to pass a special bill granting the land at Malheur to the Southern Paiutes.

Few people know more about courage than a soldier who has commanded men in battle. General Howard never forgot Sarah Winnemucca's heroism in rescuing the Southern Paiutes, nor her long fight to see that her tribe received fair treatment at the hands of the federal government. In his book, *Famous Indian Chiefs I Have Known,* Howard wrote about Sarah Winnemucca.

"If I could tell you but a tenth part of all she willingly did to help the white settlers and her own people to live peaceably together," he declared, "you would think as I do that the name of Thocmetony should have a place beside the name of Pocahontas in the history of our country."

Part II

A Passion for Justice

Justice is a word that has probably inspired more acts of courage than any other word in the human vocabulary, including war. But the dispensing of justice, like the waging of war, is not usually associated with women, except in Greek mythology.

The ancient Greeks believed that a goddess founded the first court. Her name was Athena, and she was the daughter of Zeus, the most powerful god, and Metis, the wisest goddess. Statues and paintings of Athena are a favorite motif for courthouses. You've probably seen her in front of one of them, wearing a blindfold and holding aloft the scales of justice.

The administration of justice in courtrooms, however, is only one small part of that large word *justice*. The goddess Athena also presided over the nation's welfare and was charged with guarding its intellectual and moral integrity.

I find it interesting that the ancient Greeks assigned such a role to a woman. Mythology is surprisingly rich with intuitive truths, and this, I think, is one of them. Certainly American women have shown their readiness to fight for this wider meaning of the word *justice*. They have often sensed instinctively what a great many men were unable to see— injustice is a kind of sickness, a wasting disease that eats away at the nation's moral health.

Why have women been so sensitive to injustice? Some feminists maintain that it is because they have been among its chief victims, but I think there is more to it.

Until recently, women have been outsiders in some of the most important areas of human endeavor—medicine, law, government. Even when they did succeed in making inroads into these fields, they seldom achieved positions of leadership. But the very fact that they were *not* engaged in designing and building the wheels that helped make the country go round gave them a distinct advantage in evaluating the machinery's performance.

People who become too deeply involved in running things tend to lose their perspective on them. Part of it is the old "not being able to see the forest for the trees" syndrome, but there are other complicating factors. Even in a democratic society, the existing power structure tends to become entrenched in its own ideas. The same people stay in control, the same attitudes and policies prevail.

Establishments do change, of course. Reformers, an opposition party, a sharp swing in public opinion, can turn the ins into outs almost overnight. Inevitably, a new power structure is set up, but in the past, at least, there was one thing you could always be sure of: women were still among the outs.

The majority of American females couldn't have cared less, I'm sure. Others did care and began thinking of ways to remedy the situation. Still others took advantage of their status—or lack of it—to speak out on some issues that were endangering the nation's integrity. As outsiders, they could see the injustices with greater clarity; they could also attack them with greater conviction. They had nothing to gain from their zeal—no hope of winning better jobs, higher offices, more secure positions in the establishment. Most of them, in fact, had a great deal to lose, but they spoke out anyway. Defying the power structure for justice's sake, they demonstrated a new brand of feminine courage—a courage that was not afraid to look some of the most important men in the country in the eye and say, "You're wrong."

Connecticut Learns a Lesson

One of the earliest examples of the feminine passion for justice is Prudence Crandall, the first woman to try to win equal treatment for black Americans in our schools.

I don't think it's an accident that Prudence Crandall was a Quaker. Long before the Revolution, Quaker women were grafting onto the tradition of physical courage the spiritual energy that eventually flowered into an independent tradition of moral courage. They invaded the rigid religious precincts of New England and endured whippings, brandings, and even hangings to testify to their vision of God.

From its beginning, women were accepted as full-fledged members of the Society of Friends and were permitted not only to speak at meetings but to travel as missionaries to other congregations. Women and men participated equally in Quaker "concerns"—discussions of moral issues such as the refusal to bear arms in a war and the problem of owning slaves. As early as 1754, Quaker John Woolman of New Jersey had aroused vigorous debate and earnest soul searching in meetings throughout America with his *Some Considerations on the Keeping of Negroes.* In 1776, the Society voted to expel its slaveholding members.

Prudence Crandall had decided early in life that she wanted to be a teacher. She didn't really have much choice. In those days—the early 1800s—teaching was the only profession open to women. After graduating from the New England Friends' Boarding School in Providence, she taught for a while at a girls' school in Plainfield, Connecticut. Then, in 1831, the twenty-seven-year-old teacher received a flattering offer. A committee of distinguished citizens invited her to open a boarding school in her home town of Canterbury, a few miles away.

Canterbury was the early nineteenth-century equivalent of a Scarsdale or a Grosse Pointe—an attractive and affluent community in which all the residents took great pride. The town's focal point was a large, meticulously kept green. It stood at the intersection of two major turnpikes. On one side was a handsome white-steepled Congregational to open a boarding school in her home town of Canterbury's well-to-do.

Among these, few were as wealthy as Andrew T. Judson. He had made a great deal of money from practicing law and he was also a power in state and local politics. But if Canterbury was proud of Andrew T. Judson, the rich lawyer was equally proud of Canterbury. Determined to keep up with such larger communities as Hartford and New Haven, Judson had helped raise money for a town library and pushed for the creation of a girls' school. Not only had he been instrumental in choosing Prudence Crandall as its first principal, he had also had a hand in selecting the school's site—a spacious house facing the town green, directly across the road from his own home.

When the Canterbury Female Boarding School opened in the fall of 1831, Andrew T. Judson felt justly proud of his accomplishment. The new school was a fine addition to Canterbury's social and intellectual standing, and

CORNELL UNIVERSITY

This portrait of Prudence Crandall is a study in Quaker tranquillity and inner strength.

the new principal was a model of intelligence, character, and tact. No one dreamed that within two years she would be the most hated person in town.

Just about the time that Prudence was starting her school, a Boston editor named William Lloyd Garrison was launching a new movement called Abolitionism. Until the Abolitionists appeared on the scene, the principal champion of blacks in the United States was the American Colonization Society. Founded in 1816, the society had branches in every state and numbered among its supporters such prominent Americans as James Monroe, Francis Scott Key, Henry Clay, and Andrew Jackson. The Colonizationists opposed slavery, but they wanted to free the Negroes and send them back to Africa. They had already raised enough money to purchase the colony of Liberia on Africa's west coast and had bought several thousand slaves and sent them over to settle it.

Most liberal-minded people applauded the Colonizationists' efforts, so it was something of a shock when the Abolitionists began showering them with abuse. The reformers insisted that colonization was a plot to get all the Negroes out of the country. They argued, instead, for the immediate abolition of slavery and the "amalgamation" of blacks into American society. These were radical ideas for the times, and the Abolitionists compounded their wild-eyed image by demanding equal education for free Negroes as well.

To most Americans, this last idea was almost as shocking as the instant abolition of slavery. Although by 1831 northern states had outlawed slavery, they made life unpleasant for the relatively few free blacks—about 150,000— within their borders. Freedmen could not vote in a number of states, including Connecticut, and they had to send their children to segregated public schools which a newspaperman of the time described as "nearly all, if not all, old buildings, generally in filthy and degraded neighborhoods." There were anti-Negro riots in Cincinnati, Philadelphia, Utica, and New York, and a British visitor wrote with only slight exaggeration that northern blacks were "pariahs, debarred from every fellowship save with their own despised race."

As a Quaker, Prudence Crandall deplored this situation. She read William Lloyd Garrison's fiery editorials and articles in his Abolitionist newspaper, *The Liberator,* with a rush of emotion. Inevitably, she asked herself what she could do to join this moral crusade.

Her answer came from a seventeen-year-old black girl named Sarah Harris, who was a frequent visitor in Prudence Crandall's household. She was a friend of Prudence's maid, Marcia. A respectable young woman and a devout church member, Sarah lived on her parents' farm on the outskirts of Canterbury. She was a bright girl who might well have gone to the Female Boarding School. But that was only for white girls. As soon as Sarah learned to read and write at a public school, she had taken a job as a servant for a local family.

Prudence Crandall made friends with Sarah Harris and soon discovered that she would have preferred to continue her education and become a teacher. "It is never too late to go back to school, Sarah," Prudence Crandall said.

"It is too late for me."

The sadness on Sarah's face made Prudence ignore the virtue for which she was named. Without even a breath of hesitation, she replied: "There is a place for you in my school. Will you take it?"

Prudence was deeply moved by the eagerness with which Sarah accepted her offer. The girl's response was proof that black Americans deserved equal education.

The new student had barely completed her first day at Canterbury Female Boarding School when the town was buzzing with the news. Several parents came to Miss Crandall and warned her that there would be trouble unless "the nigger girl" withdrew at once. Prudence ignored the warnings and Sarah continued her studies. Before long, the wife of the town's Episcopal minister appeared on the Crandall doorstep. She had no time to waste on chitchat. Her message was brief and to the point. "If you keep that girl," she said ominously, "you'll soon find yourself without any school."

Like many Quakers, Prudence Crandall gave the impression of being meek and mild. But her answer to this threat belied her gentle manner. The schoolmistress's eyes blazed, her lips pursed determinedly. "Then so be it," she said, "for I shall not turn her out."

To the citizens of Canterbury, it seemed like a simple matter to dismiss a single black pupil. To Prudence Crandall, the idea was unthinkable. Given a choice, she would rather keep Sarah Harris and let her white pupils go. In fact, the more she thought about that idea, the better she liked it.

On January 18, 1833, she wrote a letter to William Lloyd Garrison: "If you consider it possible to obtain 20 or 25 young ladies of color to enter this school for the term of one year at the rate of $25 per quarter, including board, washing, and tuition, I will come to Boston in a few days and make some arrangements about it."

If the residents of Canterbury were in an uproar about letting their daughters go to school with a black girl, it was easy to foresee how they would react if Prudence Crandall dismissed her white students and turned the entire school over to blacks. With understandable caution, she begged Garrison to keep her plan a secret. "If it was known," she wrote, "I have no reason to expect but it would ruin my present school."

William Lloyd Garrison's reply was encouraging, and less than two weeks later, Prudence Crandall took the stagecoach to Boston to meet him. She came away with the editor's blessing and the names of several black families who might be interested in letting her educate their daughters.

Prudence Crandall must have had more than a few qualms about what she was doing. Other advocates of black education had met with a variety of unpleasant fates. When a group of Abolitionists tried to start a school for Negro boys in New Haven, the city fathers barred it by law. In New Hampshire, when the trustees of the Canaan Academy offered their building to some Abolitionists who wanted to start a black school, several hundred outraged citizens marched on the academy. Using a hundred yoke of oxen, they dragged the building from its foundation and dumped it into a nearby lot. What would the residents of Canterbury do about Prudence Crandall's school? The young teacher was about to find out.

In February, Prudence Crandall dismissed her white students, and on March 2, a notice appeared in *The Liberator*. It announced that, "Beginning on the first Monday in April," the school owned by Miss Prudence Crandall of Canterbury, Connecticut, would be open "for the reception of young ladies and little misses of color."

The reaction in Canterbury was swift and shrill. A committee of local residents, organized by Andrew Judson, soon called on Prudence Crandall. In addition to his reputation as a lawyer and politician, Judson was a prominent supporter of the American Colonization Society. He was not only one of Canterbury's wealthiest citizens, his wife was the town's leading hostess. Normally a good-natured and witty man, Andrew Judson loved to tease his spouse about her social pretensions. There was a story told around Windham County that he once invited her down to their parlor to receive a caller and, when she appeared, solemnly introduced her to a large frog that had hopped in the front door.

Andrew Judson was neither good-natured nor witty

now. Prudence Crandall's school was just across the green from his house, and the prospect of having black neighbors filled him with indignation. He spent the better part of an hour denouncing the proposed school and condemning Prudence Crandall for trying to turn Canterbury into a center of "nigger" education.

The committee's arguments have a strangely familiar ring for twentieth-century Americans. Real estate values would plummet. Women and children would no longer be safe on the streets. Canterbury would become a ghost town. At the same time, they hastened to add that they had no objection to educating Negroes, they just wanted to see it done someplace else.

Prudence Crandall listened politely to the committee's fulminations and then made it quite clear that she was not going to change her mind. She quoted the Bible and the Declaration of Independence and reminded her visitors that Moses had had a black wife. The last remark drove them into an even worse frenzy. The rumor soon spread that Prudence Crandall was planning to take in black girls and marry them off to the town's white bachelors.

The irate citizens of Canterbury called a town meeting "to devise and adopt such measures as would effectually avert the nuisance, or speedily abate it if it should be brought into the village." The meetinghouse was next to the Congregational Church, just across the green from Miss Crandall's school. But Prudence lived up to her first name this time and elected not to attend. Instead, she asked Samuel J. May, a Unitarian minister from the town of Brooklyn, six miles away, to represent her.

Earlier, May had written her a note offering his support in her struggle. Now he appeared in Miss Crandall's parlor and listened to her plan for settling her dispute with her neighbors. Since her school was on the town green, right in the center of the most desirable residential area, she could understand part of their objection. She had decided that if the townspeople would agree to buy the building and give her time to find a new place, she would offer to move to a less conspicuous part of Canterbury.

Samuel May never got a chance to speak at the town meeting. He was shouted down when he tried to take the floor and treated to a blistering attack by Andrew Judson, who called him, among other things, a foreigner and interloper who was trying to interfere in the town's affairs. The meeting ended with cheers of support for Andrew Judson and a unanimous vote to take whatever measures were necessary to close down the "nigger" school.

A few days later, Judson, who had always been on friendly terms with May, went to the nearby town of Brooklyn to apologize for his rude behavior at the meeting. "I have nothing against either you or Miss Crandall," he explained, "but I'm deeply concerned about what these Abolitionist notions are going to do to Canterbury."

The minister assured Judson that he had nothing to worry about. "If you had allowed me to speak at the meeting," he said, "you would have found that Miss Crandall is anxious to settle the matter peaceably. She's perfectly willing to move from the town green and set up her school in a more secluded part of town."

Andrew Judson greeted the offer with an icy stare. "Mr. May," he said testily, "my friends and I are not merely opposed to the establishment of that school in Canterbury, we mean there shall be no such school anywhere in the state of Connecticut!"

The statement was nothing less than a declaration of war. When Samuel May reported it to Prudence Crandall, she nodded slowly. Her principles were about to be tested against all the power and prestige of the most influential man in Canterbury. Like most men, Mr. May prided himself on being a realist. He wondered aloud if it might be better to wait a year and let local passions cool.

More than a hundred years later, in 1948, I heard my father get the same kind of advice from well-meaning friends when he submitted his civil rights program to Congress. They told him he was going too far; he would lose southern votes and the presidency. He declined to back down on his program, which historians now call the first important breakthrough to genuine equality for America's black citizens. It took courage to risk the loss of the world's most powerful job, but my father had several generations of prominent Americans to support him. Presidents from Abraham Lincoln to Franklin D. Roosevelt had issued calls for racial justice. In 1831, Prudence Crandall could look to no such tradition. She did not even have the consolation of knowing that if she lost her fight, she would still be remembered in the history books. I am sure Dad would have agreed with me when I say that Prudence Crandall displayed more courage than any President in the struggle for Negro civil rights when she quietly answered the well-meaning Samuel May.

"Mr. May," she said, "my school will reopen on the first Monday in April."

With a dozen Negro girls in the classroom, the Canterbury Female Boarding School opened on schedule. Another dozen girls were expected within the week. Most of them lived in Boston and Providence, but some came from as far away as Philadelphia and New York.

Except for the color of their skins, the new students were not much different from the old ones. They were well-dressed, well-mannered girls who seemed to pose little threat to the peace and prosperity of Canterbury. But the town fathers were still fuming.

Andrew Judson began politicking with his cronies

in Hartford to get the state legislature to pass a law against the school. In the meantime, Canterbury's town fathers dug up an old Pauper and Vagrancy Law that had been passed back in the early days of the colony. It provided that anyone who was not a legal resident of Canterbury should pay a fine of $1.67 or leave town within ten days. The penalty for refusing to obey the law was "to be whipped on the naked body not exceeding ten stripes."

The old law was revived and invoked against one of Prudence Crandall's students, a seventeen-year-old girl from Providence, but Samuel May paid her fine and the case was dropped.

The residents of Canterbury soon found other ways to harass Prudence Crandall and her students. The town's storekeepers made an agreement not to do business with them; the stagecoach driver refused to take them as passengers. The town doctor let it be known that he would not treat them, and the minister of the Congregational Church barred them from his services.

Taking their cue from their elders, the town's teenagers devised a few tricks of their own. Crowds of boys regularly threw stones and rotten eggs at the schoolhouse, smeared mud on the fence posts and front steps, and, as a final insult, hurled manure down the well.

Prudence Crandall went on teaching. Some merchants in the neighboring town of Packerville agreed to sell her food and supplies; a Negro driver from Norwich offered to transport her pupils; and two churches, the Baptist Church in Packerville and the Friends' Meeting at Black Hill, invited them to their Sunday services.

The manure-filled well was Prudence's most serious problem. She tried, without success, to borrow fresh water from her neighbors and finally turned to her father, Pardon Crandall, for help. At the risk of becoming as much of a pariah as his daughter, he agreed to lug several pails of water a day from his own house on the far side of town to the school.

On May 24, 1833, the Connecticut legislature finally passed the eagerly awaited "Black Law." The news brought cheers and shouts of glee to Canterbury. The church bells were rung, and the Revolutionary War cannon on the village green boomed out a thirteen-gun salute. The law made it illegal for anyone to "set up or establish in this State any school, academy, or literary institution for the instruction or education of colored persons who are not inhabitants of this State. . . ." The woman it was aimed at, Prudence Crandall, was immediately served notice that it would be strictly enforced.

A few days later, the sheriff of Windham County appeared at Prudence Crandall's school with a warrant for her arrest. She was brought before Judge Rufus Adams, charged with violating a statute of the state of Connecticut, and ordered to stand trial at the County Court in Brooklyn on August 22. As an added humiliation, the judge decreed that unless one of her friends stepped forward to post bond, she would have to remain in jail until her case came to court.

The schoolmistress's Abolitionist friends would gladly have posted the bond that would have kept her out of jail. But Prudence Crandall refused their offers. She was ready to suffer for her beliefs and she wanted everyone in Connecticut to know it.

Showing a natural instinct for public relations, Samuel May decided to turn Prudence Crandall into a martyr. He arranged for her to be put in a cell that had previously been occupied by a man who was hanged for strangling his wife. The cell was thoroughly scrubbed and aired, a new bed with fresh linens was installed, and a young girl from Brooklyn,

Mary Benson, was enlisted to keep the schoolmistress company.

Even so, the prospect of occupying a murderer's cell could not have been very appealing. Suspecting that Prudence might have second thoughts about her decision, Samuel May arrived as the sheriff was taking her into the jailhouse and told her that it was still not too late to post the bond that would secure her release. Prudence shook her head. She bade May and the handful of other friends who had come to lend their support a cordial good night and went off to her cell.

Although she was released the next day, Prudence Crandall's imprisonment had, as Samuel May had foreseen, aroused a wave of public sympathy for her cause. Many people who had remained silent now spoke out in favor of the school and began condemning Andrew Judson and his friends for persecuting its principal. Prudence soon discovered that she had other allies as well. Arthur Tappan, a New York merchant and philanthropist and one of the founders of the American Anti-Slavery Society, not only offered to pay her legal expenses but also put up the money to establish a local newspaper, *The Unionist,* to defend her against the attacks of the pro-Colonizationist newspapers in the area.

Prudence Crandall's case went before the County Court on August 22. Her attorneys argued that Connecticut's Black Law was unconstitutional. They contended that a state law could not contradict the U. S. Constitution, which guaranteed the citizens of one state privileges and immunities in all the others. The prosecution countered with the argument that blacks were not entitled to these privileges, because they were not citizens. Although the presiding judge decided that the law was constitutional, the jurors were unable to agree, and the case was passed on to the Superior Court.

The second trial began on October 3. This time Prudence Crandall was convicted of violating the Black Law, but her attorney insisted that an error had been made in presenting the evidence and persuaded the judge to let them appeal the case to the Court of Errors.

The court did not meet until the following summer. In the meantime, Prudence Crandall continued to run her school. She had already complied with the Black Law and sent her out-of-state students home, but she still had an enrollment of seventeen black girls from various parts of Connecticut.

The harassments and threats continued, too. Prudence Crandall bore them stoically and even urged her students to try to understand and forgive their persecutors.

On July 22, 1834, Prudence Crandall's long ordeal appeared to be over. The Court of Errors overturned the verdict of the Superior Court and quashed her case for lack of evidence. A month later, she married the Reverend Calvin Philleo, a Baptist minister from Ithaca, New York. But her hopes of staying in Canterbury and continuing to run the Female Boarding School were soon crushed.

When the school opened in September, a new and more dangerous round of assaults began. First, the building was set on fire. Fortunately, the blaze did not spread and was quickly extinguished. Then, a few nights later, a group of men armed with heavy iron bars stole up to the school, stationed themselves around it, and, at a signal, smashed every window.

That was about all that the Reverend Mr. Philleo wanted to see of Canterbury. He informed Prudence that he had a "call" from a church in New York and was planning to move there. As a good wife, she must accompany him. Reluctantly, Prudence agreed that the situation in Canterbury made future education a dubious proposition. The next day, the students were told that the school was closing, and they packed their trunks and went home. The Philleos departed for New York a week later.

In 1886, fifty-two years after she had left the state, the Connecticut legislature publicly apologized to Prudence Crandall Philleo. They offered to return her schoolhouse and to compensate her with an annual pension of four hundred dollars. Prudence, now eighty-three but still lively, refused the house. Briskly, she told the legislators that she was now comfortable and independent in Elk Falls, Kansas, in a "little pioneer box house of three rooms." But she did accept the annuity as payment of a "just debt" owed to her by the state of Connecticut for destroying her "hopes and prospects . . . by an unjust and unconstitutional law."

Prudence Crandall lost her fight. Or did she? One of the most remarkable things about courage is the way it inspires others to imitate its example. This is what happened in Canterbury, Connecticut, and the surrounding county of Windham. Within thirty years of Prudence's defeat, the area emerged as a center of the antislavery movement. The infamous Black Law quietly disappeared, and Connecticut became one of the first states to grant Negroes the rights and privileges of free men.

People do learn, they do change; slowly, reluctantly. But it only happens when someone with courage leads the way.

The Woman Who Killed
Judge Lynch

Most of us have never seen a mob in action. A glimpse of
one in Canterbury was enough to frighten Prudence Crandall's husband into the next state. But that Connecticut
crowd of window breakers and arsonists were models of
nonviolence compared to a lynch mob. For sheer terror mas-
querading as instant justice, lynchers are in a class by themselves. To stand up to them takes courage with a capital C.
I'm proud to say that more than a few Americans have displayed this kind of courage, but I'm prouder still that one
of the first and fiercest enemies of this ugly national phenomenon was a woman.

Ida Wells was the daughter of slaves. Her mother,
Lizzie Bell, had been sold for the first time when she was
only seven years old. By the time Lizzie Bell was a young
woman she had belonged to a half dozen owners. Ida's father,
James Wells, was more fortunate. He had only one master,
and the man, who was also his father, cared enough about
his illegitimate son to apprentice him to a carpenter so he
could learn the trade.

As it happened, Lizzie Bell was a cook in the carpenter's household. She and James Wells, the young ap-

prentice, fell in love and were married. Ida, their first child, was born in Holly Springs, Mississippi, on July 16, 1862.

Six months later, President Abraham Lincoln signed the Emancipation Proclamation. The historic document did not substantially change James and Lizzie Wells's way of life. They continued to work at the same jobs. But it did give them a new sense of hope for their children. From an early age, Ida was taught that black people were no longer objects to be bought and sold. They had freedom now, and dignity, and the right to live and work where they pleased.

One of Lizzie Bell Wells's most important dreams for her children was a decent education. She hoped to see them graduate not only from grade school but from the newly established freedmen's high school in Holly Springs. Ida had finished two years of high school when her parents and their youngest child died in a yellow fever epidemic. Their oldest daughter was left to support herself and the five surviving brothers and sisters. Ida let the hems out of her skirts, stuck a few pins in her hair, and obtained a job teaching school for twenty-five dollars a month. Although she was barely sixteen, she solemnly assured the school superintendent that she had just celebrated her eighteenth birthday.

Ida stayed at the rural school in Holly Springs until the younger Wells children were old enough to look after themselves. Then she moved to Memphis. By now an experienced teacher, she had no trouble finding work in one of the city's black schools.

Lizzie and James Wells had promised their children equality. But in the post-Civil War South, equality for blacks was rapidly becoming a meaningless concept. By the time Ida Wells arrived in Memphis in 1884, southern racists had already built up the network of repressive laws and customs that would require the Civil Rights acts of the twentieth century to tear down.

UNIVERSITY OF CHICAGO

This picture of Ida Wells-Barnett was taken not long after she wrote her exposé of lynching. For me, it is the face of a woman who has seen how ugly life can be, but is determined to fight back.

Ida had encountered little discrimination in Holly Springs. One reason may have been that she was too busy teaching school and raising her younger brothers and sisters to notice. When she moved to Memphis, however, she became bitterly aware of the indignities to which black people were being subjected. The system made a mockery of everything she had ever heard from her mother and father about equality.

Ida Wells had taken over her parents' responsibilities for her brothers and sisters in Holly Springs. In Memphis, she vowed to fight for their aspirations for a better life for all black men and women. Ida's first skirmish with the forces of prejudice occurred soon after she made that vow. She had taken the Chesapeake and Ohio Railroad from Memphis to Nashville, Tennessee, where she was attending summer classes at Fisk University. Ida had paid for a first-class ticket, but the conductor informed her that Negroes were not allowed to ride in the first-class coach; she would have to use the smoker. When Ida refused to move, the conductor summoned the baggageman, and the two of them threatened to throw her off the moving train. Ida finally retreated to the smoker, but she got off at the next stop, took another train back to Memphis, and instituted legal proceedings against the railroad.

Ida won her case in the circuit court and was awarded five hundred dollars in damages. But the decision was reversed by Tennessee's Supreme Court. Furious now, Ida only widened her fight against racial injustice. There were a number of Negro newspapers in Memphis, and she began writing articles about race and politics in the South, under the pen name "Iola." Eventually she bought a partial interest in one paper, the *Free Speech*. Although she continued to teach school, her summer vacations were devoted to travel-

ing around the South drumming up new subscribers and
signing up correspondents to send in local news.

She also continued to write. Her articles were so good
that they were regularly reprinted in black newspapers elsewhere in the country. T. Thomas Fortune, publisher of the
prestigious New York *Age,* called Ida Wells "one of the few
of our women who handle a goose quill with diamond points
as easily as any man in newspaper work. If Iola were a man,
she would be a humming independent in politics. She has
plenty of nerve, and is as sharp as a steel trap."

Ida never shied away from controversial subjects. One
day, she decided to write about a topic on which she was well
informed—Memphis's black schools. In that era of "separate
but equal" schools in the South, Negro education was always
separate but by no stretch of the imagination could it be
considered equal. In Memphis, for instance, there were not
enough schools. Those that did exist were ramshackle old
buildings badly in need of repairs. The teachers, as Ida acidly
described them, were often only slightly better educated
than their pupils. Ida knew of several who had unsavory
reputations. One had been appointed only because she was
having an affair with a member of the school board.

Ida's article appeared in the *Free Speech* unsigned,
but everyone, including the Board of Education, knew that
she had written it. When the list of teachers for the coming
school year was announced a few weeks later, Ida Wells's
name was conspicuously absent.

With school about to reopen, it was too late for Ida
to find a teaching position anywhere else, so she decided to
become a full-time newspaperwoman. She was soon earning
enough to buy a half share in the paper. Her partner, an
older and more experienced publisher named J. L. Fleming,
served as business manager while Ida handled the editing

and subscription department. *Free Speech* had originally had a circulation of about fifteen hundred. After Ida took over, it jumped to four thousand.

The Memphis *Free Speech* became more and more outspoken about the problems of southern blacks. Finally Ida took on one subject that everyone, black or white, was afraid to discuss: lynching.

In the post-Civil War years, lynching had become a steadily growing phenomenon. It had started in Virginia in the late eighteenth century. A frontier judge, Charles Lynch, had a habit of stringing up lawbreakers without bothering to give them a jury trial. The tradition had followed the frontier west. On a national scale, about one out of every three victims of a lynch mob was white. But in the South, after the Civil War, the victim was almost always black. The practice grew from a handful of incidents in the 1860s and '70s to epidemic proportions in the 1880s. When Ida became editor of the *Free Speech* in 1892, the average had reached an appalling two hundred a year.

The usual excuses for lynching were rape of a white woman or murder of a white man. Ida had often wondered how well the charges would have stood up if they had been presented in a court of law. It occurred to her that lynching might be a convenient way to establish white supremacy and keep blacks in their places. She soon had a chance to confirm her suspicions in a very unpleasant way.

Among her many friends in Memphis was a young couple named Tommie and Betty Moss. A friendly, outgoing man, Tommie was a letter carrier for the Memphis post office. His route included the offices of the *Free Speech*, and he always had a few tidbits of news to pass along when he got there.

Anxious to earn more than his meager postman's salary, Tommie had saved his money and with two partners,

Calvin McDowell and Henry Stewart, invested in a grocery store. The People's Grocery Company was located in a predominantly black neighborhood known as the Curve. It had gotten its name because the trolley-car tracks curved sharply at that point. Most of the residents of the Curve knew Tommie Moss from either his church or his lodge. They quickly abandoned the white grocer with whom they usually traded and began shopping at Tommie's. The People's Grocery Company was soon doing a thriving business, and the only one at the Curve who wasn't delighted with its success was the white grocer whose trade had fallen off.

One day a group of black boys who lived at the Curve got into a fight with a group of white boys from a few blocks away. The white storekeeper's son was involved in the fracas. When he arrived home covered with cuts and bruises, his irate father stomped out to thrash the boys who had beaten him up.

The dispute soon erupted into a full-scale brawl between white and black fathers. When the black men won, the white grocer was so angry that he swore out a warrant for their arrest. The case was settled quickly with the blacks paying minuscule fines, but the word soon got around that the whites planned to take further revenge by raiding the People's Grocery Company the following Saturday night.

Tommie Moss's store was outside the city limits, so he had no hope of getting police protection. Instead, he asked several of his friends to stand guard that evening in case the attack materialized.

Saturday night was, as usual, quite busy. Shortly before ten o'clock, Tommie Moss was going over his accounts for the week and Calvin McDowell was waiting on the last of the evening's customers. Suddenly shots rang out from the rear of the store. A group of white men had broken in through the back door, and Tommie Moss's guards had fired on them. Tommie raced out into the alley behind the store and found three white men lying wounded on the ground.

Tommie's friends had fired in self-defense, but the account that appeared in the Memphis newspapers gave no hint of that fact. According to the story, the three wounded men were police officers who had been tracking down a gang of criminals hiding in the People's Grocery Company. The store was described as "a low dive" and "a resort of thieves and thugs." Only one item in the newspaper story was accurate. All three owners of the grocery store had been jailed, and they could expect no mercy if the "officers" died.

Even before the newspapers appeared on the stands, a squadron of policemen surged through the Curve looking for any blacks who might have taken part in the shooting. Over a hundred men were dragged from their homes and thrown in jail on charges of suspicion.

Memphis's Negroes were both angry and fearful, but they were primarily concerned about Tommie Moss and his partners. Although lynchings were relatively unknown in Memphis, the story of the shootings had been so wildly distorted that there might well be some retaliation, especially if the wounded men died.

A group of prominent Negroes decided to mount a watch at the county jail. The guards included a state legislator and a city councilman, assisted by a troop of black militia known as the Tennessee Rifles. The watch continued for forty-eight hours. On Tuesday morning, the wounded men were pronounced out of danger and there was a visible decline in tension between blacks and whites. The volunteer guards, convinced that the prisoners had no further need for protection, went home.

That night, a group of white men broke into the jail

and removed Tommie Moss, Calvin McDowell, and Henry Stewart from their cells. The three men were bundled onto a railway car, taken out to the countryside, and shot.

The lynching was no small and clandestine operation. It had been organized by some of the most influential men in Memphis. The city's leading newspaper, the *Commercial Appeal*, delayed its morning edition to print the story, and from the details that were included, it was obvious that the reporter had either witnessed the slaying or talked to one of the mob.

Tommie Moss was said to have begged to be spared for the sake of his little daughter and his wife, who was pregnant with their second child. Calvin McDowell had grabbed one of the lyncher's guns and refused to let go. McDowell's right hand had been blasted away, and his eyes were gouged out.

In the wake of the lynchings, Memphis's blacks, who had every reason to be in a vengeful mood, remained calm. But the incidents unleashed a torrent of white rage. The sheriff stationed armed guards at the Curve with orders to shoot down any Negro who tried to make trouble. Another group of lawmen took possession of the People's Grocery Company, helping themselves to whatever they wanted and destroying everything they couldn't eat or steal. A few days later, the store and what was left of its contents were sold at auction. The white grocer had effectively destroyed his competition.

Ida Wells had been in Natchez on a business trip when the lynchings occurred. As soon as she arrived home, she sat down and wrote a searing denunciation of the event, focusing most of her anger on the city of Memphis.

"There is nothing we can do about the lynching now," she said. "There is only one thing left that we can do; save our money and leave a town which will neither protect our lives and property, nor give us a fair trial in the courts, but takes us out and murders us in cold blood when accused by white persons."

Before he died, Tommie Moss was reported to have made a statement urging his people to go west because there was no justice for blacks in Tennessee. Ida repeated the plea in her editorial. The result was a massive exodus from Memphis. The pastors of two large Negro churches migrated to Oklahoma, taking their entire congregations with them. Hundreds of other black families followed, and the city soon began to feel the financial loss. Clothing and furniture stores suffered sharp declines in business, housewives were unable to find maids, and there was a noticeable slowdown in the use of public transportation.

Ida was secretly delighted at the economic havoc the black migration was causing, but she feigned innocence when the treasurer of the City Railway Company came to call on her. He had heard, the man explained, that "the colored people" had given up riding the streetcars because they were afraid of electricity. "Why don't you run a story telling them there's no danger?" he asked.

Ida pretended to be puzzled. The electric trolley lines had been installed more than six months ago but the treasurer had only just noticed a decline in fares. "When did it start?" she asked.

"About six weeks ago," the man told her, "and we're losing a fortune. If I can't get things back to normal, I'm going to be out of a job."

Ida could have made a nasty comment on the fact that the man's main interest was saving his own position. Instead, she pointed out that the lynchings had taken place about six weeks ago.

"But our company didn't have anything to do with that," he sputtered. "Our owners are northern capitalists."

"Yes," retorted Ida, "but your managers are southern lynchers. Every white man in town knew about that lynching, and not one of them did anything to protect those boys."

The man looked uncomfortable.

"No finer, cleaner man than Tommie Moss ever walked the streets of Memphis," Ida went on. "The colored people feel that every white man in Memphis who consented to his death is as guilty as those who fired the guns that took his life. That's why they're not riding your streetcars. And the nickels and dimes they're saving will go to pay their way out of this miserable city."

"Why don't you people find the lynchers yourselves?" the man suggested.

Ida laughed harshly. "As if we could," she said. "I have heard that the criminal court judge himself was one of them. Would a grand jury ever do anything to him? And would the reporter from the *Appeal* be made to tell what he saw? Somehow, I doubt it."

When the treasurer of the railway company left, Ida couldn't resist writing an article about his visit. She ended the piece by urging her readers to continue boycotting the streetcars.

The black exodus from Memphis continued. The first stop on the journey west was the ferry across the Mississippi. Ida was amused by one old man who started up the gangplank with his dog. Halfway up, the dog stopped dead in his tracks. His master tugged and tugged at his leash and finally said, "What you want to stay back there for? Want the white folks to lynch you too?"

In an effort to halt the Negro departures, Memphis's white newspapers began running stories about the hardships out West. They told lurid tales of hostile Indians, dreadful weather, and fatal diseases. Ida retaliated by going out West herself. She spent three weeks traveling through

Oklahoma, where most of the blacks had settled, and returned with a firsthand report of conditions there.

By now, Ida Wells was not very popular among the
white citizens of Memphis. There was a real possibility that
she might be lynched herself. Some of her friends urged her
to give up her outspoken editorials, but Ida refused. Instead, she bought a small pistol. "I felt that one had better
die fighting against injustice than to die like a dog or a rat
in a trap," she said. "I had already determined to sell my
life as dearly as possible if attacked. I felt if I could take
one lyncher with me, this would even up the score a little
bit."

In the weeks since Tommie Moss and his partners
had been killed, Ida had been doing some serious thinking
about lynching. The usual excuse was that the lynchers
were outraged over the crime which the Negro had supposedly committed. They often conceded that the lynching
was a violation of law and order, but they invariably pointed
out that the victim was a vicious criminal who didn't deserve
mercy anyway.

Like most whites and blacks, Ida had accepted the
argument that the lynchers acted out of rage and the victims
deserved their fate. Now that she had a firsthand report of
a lynching and knew all the circumstances, she began to
doubt this standard explanation. Tommie Moss and his
friends had been lynched solely because of a business rivalry.

Ida began investigating other lynchings. She read
the stories that appeared in the newspapers and talked to
witnesses. She soon saw that there was far more to the problem than met the eye. In the first place, most of the lynchings did not involve rape. They were for a variety of charges,
ranging from "conjuring" to "being saucy." Those that were
for rape often became that only when they were reported to
the public. Typical was the case that Ida tracked down in

Tunica County, Mississippi. An Associated Press report of the lynching said that the man had raped a seven-year-old girl. Ida found out that the girl was actually a grown woman, that she had gone to the Negro's cabin on her own, and that her father had led the lynch mob in order to save his daughter's reputation.

Ida began to realize that lynching served a very definite purpose. It provided an excuse to terrorize Negroes, especially those who were acquiring wealth and property. It was all part of a general effort to "keep the nigger down."

Tommie Moss and his companions had been lynched on March 9. For the next two months, Ida collected details on dozens of other lynchings. She traveled throughout the South, from Texas to Virginia, asking white and black men to tell her the facts in each case. To call this dangerous work is an understatement. Imagine a lone black woman in some small town in Alabama or Mississippi, asking questions no one wanted to answer about a crime that half the whites in the town had committed. More than once, Ida Wells thought she would have to use her small pistol in self-defense and as a result would become one more victim of lynch law. But courage has a tendency to intimidate cowards. Ida returned from her fact-finding expedition with enough ammunition to start a war against lynchers.

The first misconception she decided to correct was the one about rape. On May 25, 1892, the front page of the *Free Speech* carried the following story:

"Eight Negroes lynched since last issue of the *Free Speech*. Three were charged with killing white men and five with raping white women. Nobody in this section believes the old thread-bare lie that Negro men assault white women. If Southern white men are not careful they will over-reach themselves and a conclusion will be reached which will be very damaging to the moral reputation of their women."

The editorial appeared on a Saturday. The following Monday it was reprinted on the editorial page of the *Commercial Appeal*. Beneath it was a message calling on the white men of Memphis to avenge this insult to the honor of their women: "The black wretch who had written that foul lie should be tied to a stake at the corner of Main and Madison Streets, a pair of tailor's shears used on him, and he should then be burned at the stake."

Unaware of the menacing atmosphere building up in Memphis, Ida had departed for Philadelphia to cover a church conference. From there, she took another train to New York to confer with T. Thomas Fortune, editor of the New York *Age*. Fortune was hoping to persuade her to join his paper as a full-time staff reporter.

Ida stepped off the train expecting a jovial greeting from a man who had expressed so much admiration for her work. Instead, Fortune looked like he was on his way to the funeral of a good friend. His words were even more baffling. "I've been trying to get you to New York for a long time," he said. "And now that you're here, I'm afraid you'll have to stay."

Ida asked him what he was talking about. Fortune produced a copy of the New York *Sun* with an Associated Press dispatch from Memphis. It told how a mob of angry white men had gathered in front of the Cotton Exchange in downtown Memphis. There were shouts of "Let's get that black bastard," and "Let's show the niggers." The mob had marched to the offices of the *Free Speech* on Hernando Street and wrecked the building. They smashed the printing press and the furniture and left a warning for the owners. If they attempted to resume publication, they would be writing their own death sentences.

Ida's first question was about the safety of the paper's business manager, J. L. Fleming. She was relieved to hear

that he had fled Memphis before the mob struck. At her
hotel, Ida found several telegrams waiting for her, begging
her not to return to Memphis. Soon, letters began pouring
in with further details. The white men had discovered that
Ida Wells was the author of the editorials and had decreed
that she was to be killed on sight. Her home was being
watched, and a gunman appeared at the railway station
every time a train from the North was due in.

Ida's friends assured her that they would do everything they could to protect her if she did decide to come
back, but Ida did not want to be responsible for any more
bloodshed. She stayed in New York.

Ida Wells might have gone back to Memphis. Did she
fail a test of courage by deciding to stay in New York? I
don't think so. Courage is not recklessness. The courageous
do not go out of their way to flirt with danger and death,
especially when it is more important for them to stay alive.
If Ida had gone back to Memphis, she would have been
killed. All the research she had done on lynching would have
died with her. A return to Memphis would have been playing into the hands of the racists.

T. Thomas Fortune offered Ida a job on the New
York *Age*. One of her first articles was a seven-column front-
page story giving the names, dates, and locations of several
dozen lynchings. In almost every case, the lynchers were
important members of the white community who could have
legally punished the wrongdoers if they had had any evidence
of their guilt, while the victims had neither the political nor
financial strength to protect themselves.

Ida's story caused a sensation in black communities
around the country. The issue sold ten thousand copies,
one thousand in Memphis alone. The distinguished black
leader Frederick Douglass congratulated her. He was well
aware that lynching was a problem, he told her, but like

most blacks he had always believed that the victims were guilty of the crimes for which they were doomed.

In the wake of the enthusiastic response to her articles, Ida took to the lecture platform. She traveled to every major city in the country, talking about the evils of lynching and organizing anti-lynching societies. No one ever refuted the mass of evidence she had accumulated. More than once, reporters in the audience squirmed when Ida condemned white newspapers in the North for complacently accepting the phony stories put out by southern editors to excuse lynchings. She told how she had gone to dozens of white papers after she was driven out of Memphis, offering them her facts to refute "the foul slander that all the Northern papers were publishing, without question, about Negro assaults on white women." Not one editor listened to her. The age of the investigative reporter had not yet dawned, but Ida Wells hastened its coming a little. "Is not the North by its seeming acquiescence as responsible morally as the South is criminally for the awful lynching record of the past thirteen years?" she asked. There was only one answer to that question.

In 1895, Ida married a Chicago attorney named Ferdinand Barnett. That same year she published *A Red Record,* the first authentic account of lynching ever compiled. It gave full details of three years of lynchings in the United States. To ensure its authenticity, Ida took all her data from white sources, and in most cases described the incidents in the exact words of the white journalists.

After her marriage, Ida gave up many of her outside interests to devote her time to raising her four children. The one cause she refused to abandon was her crusade against lynching. She served as chairman of the Anti-Lynching Bureau of the Afro-American Council, a national protest organization that was a forerunner of the NAACP. She was also a member of the delegation that called on President William McKinley in 1898 to protest the lynching of a black postmaster in South Carolina. In 1909, when a black man was lynched in southern Illinois, she went to Springfield and urged Governor Charles Deneen to reinstate the sheriff who had tried to prevent the tragedy. The Governor did so and thus helped put an end to lynching in Illinois.

In an era when blacks and even sympathetic whites were reluctant to speak out against this ultimate injustice, one woman had the courage to stir the country's conscience. Thanks to Ida Wells-Barnett's efforts, lynchings, which had reached an all-time high at the beginning of the 1890s, gradually tapered off. The lynch rate rose again after World War I. By then, the NAACP was ready to take up the crusade. But it was Ida Wells-Barnett who pointed the way.

Mother Jones Goes to War

The struggle for justice—and against injustice—on behalf of black Americans is not yet over. Perhaps that is what gives the stories of Prudence Crandall and Ida Wells-Barnett special poignancy. But the leaders of the battle for racial equality can be encouraged by the fact that another struggle for justice which began around the same time and which was almost as bitter has been successfully concluded. I mean the fight for fair wages and decent treatment for the working-man.

I say "man" because the vast majority of America's laborers have always been male. But the labor movement has never lacked female supporters. Some were identifying with injustices committed against fathers, husbands, or brothers, but others, like Leonora Barry and Rose Schneiderman, had seen firsthand the terrible exploitation of women in industry.

The fight for fair labor practices was a no-holds-barred brawl. In some places, like the steel mills and the coal mines, it became an all-out war, fought with knives, clubs, revolvers, rifles, and machine guns. Here, the women usually stayed on the sidelines—except for one courageous lady, Mary Harris Jones, who never had any qualms about wading right into the fray.

I have been alternately amused and appalled by some of Mary Jones's exploits. The amusement stems from the fact that she was the world's most unlikely-looking labor leader—a tiny, white-haired woman, who from all appearances would have been more at home sitting in a rocking chair darning socks.

I also have a special feeling for this woman of courage, because she reminds me of another woman whom I knew and loved very much, my paternal grandmother, "Mamma" Truman. She shared Mary Jones's refusal to quit and her serene disregard for old age.

Born in Cork, Ireland, in 1830, Mary Harris came to the United States as a young girl. Her father was a railroad construction worker, so the family lived in several different cities across the country. When Mary grew up, she settled in Memphis, where she married an ironworker named Jones and bore him four children.

In 1867, that scourge of nineteenth-century America, yellow fever, hit Memphis. Mary Jones's husband and children were among the victims. In the aftermath of the tragedy, the thirty-seven-year-old widow moved to Chicago and supported herself by opening a dressmaking shop.

Four years later, Mary Jones had to endure a second tragedy—the great Chicago fire. She lost her shop, her home, and all her possessions. Alone and adrift, she wandered into the charred meeting hall of the Knights of Labor one evening. She already had a moderate interest in the labor movement, developed through her late husband, a staunch member of the iron molders' union. But the spirit that made her a leader in this first attempt to forge a national labor organization flowed out of her blood.

The Irish were the first immigrant group to come to

CULVER PICTURES INC.

This is Mother Jones. It is hard to picture her putting her hand over the muzzle of a machine gun. She looks as if she is going to a prayer meeting.

America in huge numbers—a staggering 1,694,838 arrived between 1840 and 1860—and they endured savage discrimination and exploitation. Lemuel Shattuck, a census statistician, estimated that the average lifespan of an Irish immigrant in the eastern city slums was ten years. A laborer's pay, when he got it, was seldom more than $1.25 a day, and out of this meager sum he had to buy his food and clothing at stores run by the contractors who hired him. He worked from sunrise until, as one laborer put it, "our sweat mixes with the nightly dew."

Tyrone Power, a famous actor and ancestor of the late movie star, sent home the following description of Irish laborers at work in Louisiana:

> I saw hundreds of fine fellows laboring beneath the sun that even at this winter season was at times insufferably fierce and amidst a pestilential swamp whose exhalations were fetid to a degree scarcely endurable for a few months. They subsist on the coarsest fare . . . at the mercy of a hard contractor who wrings his profits from their blood; and all this for a pittance that merely enables them to exist.

One investigator estimated that twenty-five out of every one hundred Irish railroad laborers died from injuries or illnesses related to their work. Again and again, contractors would abscond with the men's wages, which led to so-called "Irish riots." At various times, the militia of Baltimore, Chicago, and New York State had to be called out to stop enraged Irishmen from tearing up their own handiwork.

Somehow, these men retained a faith in the promise of America. The proof is in the little known story of Irish "remittances"—money saved from their pitifully small wages and sent back to Ireland to bring friends and relatives to our shores. Between 1848 and 1861, these remittances totaled $59,236,555. In 1858, an English social scientist declared: "If we look back through the pages of American history to the day when the Mayflower first sighted that wild New England shore, we shall find no more magnificent spectacle than this—the work not of the great, the rich or the mighty, but of those who were destitute of all things save true hearts and strong hands."

Mary Harris Jones's sympathy for these true hearts and strong hands was sharpened by her personal experience in America. She noted that most of the yellow fever victims in Memphis had been poor people, usually Irish or black laboring men and their families. The rich could afford to flee the stricken city. In Chicago, her work as a dressmaker brought her into constant contact with the city's rich. She saw them in their plush, well-heated mansions while most of her people shivered in unheated, rickety tenements. In the summer, the lake front was a gathering place for sweltering slum dwellers desperate for a breath of cool air. The wealthy Chicagoans went off to their elaborate "cottages" at the seashore or mountains. As far as Mary Harris Jones could see, the millionaire industrialists were completely indifferent to the sufferings of the men whose labor enabled them to live so well.

Mary Harris Jones's black bonnet and shawl soon became a familiar sight at labor rallies and strike barricades. The men she befriended took to calling her Mother, a familiar term of affection in that era. Although she was passionate about every aspect of the labor movement, her main concern was the plight of America's miners. From the 1890s on, she devoted most of her efforts to their fight for better wages and working conditions and the right to join the United Mine Workers Union, which was, at the time, their only hope of changing their lives.

Mary Jones involved herself in the coal miners' fight for one simple reason—they were the ones who needed her

most. Every nineteenth-century capitalist worked his employees twelve or fourteen hours a day, six days a week. All
of them regularly ignored standards of safety and sanitation.
But the mine owners had some practices that made other
corporate barons look like model employers. The mining
districts were private property, which meant that the coal
companies exercised total control over everything that went
on there. They owned the workers' houses, usually miserable
shacks for which they charged exorbitant rents; they operated
the local stores, where again the prices were outrageous.
They provided doctors, schoolteachers, and clergymen and
taxed their workers heavily for their services. As the final
injustice, most companies paid their men in scrip, not cash,
so it was impossible for them to leave and go anywhere else.

The miners needed a union, but they were too beaten
down by their bosses to organize one. Outside organizers
who tried to enter the mining districts met with brutal opposition. Company guards, thugs, and hoodlums recruited from
the big cities greeted them with guns and clubs, which they
had no qualms about using.

Not only did Mary Harris Jones refuse to be intimidated by such tactics, she became an expert at developing
some effective, but less deadly, tactics of her own. During a
strike in Arnot, Pennsylvania, in 1900, she arrived at the
mining district to discover that the coal company had hired
scabs to take the men's places in the mines. Mother Jones
ordered the strikers to stay home but asked their wives to
meet her the next morning with their mops and brooms and
dishpans.

When the women showed up, Mother Jones placed
a wild-eyed, disheveled looking Irishwoman at their head
and marched them off to the mineshaft. The scabs and the
mules who hauled the coal carts were just getting ready to
go down the shaft when the women appeared. Up the hill

they came, beating on their dishpans, waving their mops and brooms, and yelling at the top of their lungs.

The sheriff, who was standing by to keep order, was relieved to see a bunch of housewives instead of the burly miners he had expected. He stepped up to the woman at the head of the line and said pleasantly, "My dear lady, remember the mules. Please don't frighten them."

The Irishwoman responded by whacking him in the stomach with her large tin dishpan. "To hell with you and the mules," she screamed.

The astonished sheriff tumbled down the hill into a creek. The frightened mules bucked and kicked and ran off in the opposite direction. The scabs started after them with the women in pursuit. Every time the scabs caught the mules and quieted them, a few bangs on the dishpans sent them flying again. Dishpan demonstrations became a favorite technique for discouraging scabs and disrupting mine operations.

Mother Jones remained active in the labor movement at an age when most men and women have long since retired. When she was seventy-three years old, she went out to Colorado, traveled around the copper mines disguised as a peddler, and gathered enough information to persuade the United Mine Workers to call a strike.

At eighty-one, she was still going strong, working with striking machinists of the Southern Pacific Railroad in California. But her heart remained in the coal fields of Pennsylvania and West Virginia. One morning, she read in the paper that there was a strike at one of her old stamping grounds, the Paint Creek Coal Company in West Virginia. Mother Jones canceled the rest of her speaking engagements, tied up her few possessions in a shawl, and headed back east.

The conductor on the rickety two-car train that ran between Charleston and Paint Creek told her all about the

dispute. The men who walked out had been evicted from
their homes and forced to live in tents in the nearby hills.
The coal company's guards staged frequent raids on the tent
colonies, beating the strikers and occasionally even attacking their wives and children. The same guards patrolled the
roads that led into the district. "Don't go up there," the
conductor warned Mother Jones. "They have machine guns
set up along the highway and they don't care who they kill."

Mother Jones ignored the warning. When the train
pulled into Paint Creek Junction, she was the first one off.
Three armed guards were lounging on the platform. They
eyed her suspiciously, but Mother Jones gave them only a
passing glance. She was busy looking up at the hills, where
the striking miners had fled. A young boy, who recognized
her from one of her previous visits to Paint Creek, approached her.

"Mother Jones," he said eagerly, "have you come to
stay?"

"Yes," she replied, "I've come to stay."

One of the guards straightened up. "Mother Jones?"
he inquired, with dismay.

Mother Jones nodded. "That's what they call me."

The boy offered to guide Mother Jones to the tent
colony. Along the way, he told her about his own experiences
in the strike. Company guards had driven his father out of
the mining district. "They beat us, too," he said solemnly,
pulling down his worn cotton shirt to expose the ugly welts
on his narrow shoulders. "My mother's back looks even
worse."

Within the hour, Mother Jones was sitting in one
of the canvas tents listening to further tales of horror. She
met widows whose husbands had been shot down by guards,
children who had seen their mothers clubbed with the
butts of guns. Exhausted and disheartened, the men in the

hills were on the verge of giving up. An old man whose son had been killed by the guards shook his head. "I think the strike is lost," he said sadly.

Mary Harris Jones's gray eyes flashed behind her silver-rimmed spectacles, her chin jutted out defiantly. "No it isn't!" she snapped. "It's not lost until your souls are lost!"

The eighty-one-year-old dynamo took charge. She traveled up and down Paint Creek, stopping at every cluster of tents. Her presence renewed the men's sagging spirits. More important, she had a plan. She organized three thousand miners and led them in a march over the hills to Charleston to deliver an ultimatum to West Virginia's Governor. They demanded that he outlaw the coal company's guards and replace them with state militia, who would be responsible to the government of West Virginia and not to the mine operators. The Governor agreed, and the removal of the hated gunmen encouraged the strikers to hold out.

Not long after that, a young miner from another district called Cabin Creek appeared at the Paint Creek tent colony looking for Mother Jones. "We're hoping you'll come over and talk to us," he told her. "I've already been to Charleston and tried to get some of the national officers to come, but they all said no. They don't want to get killed."

Cabin Creek was notorious for its dreadful working conditions, but the union had been stymied in its efforts to do anything about them. Every labor organizer who went there was beaten up and either thrown into the creek or tossed into some desolate ravine. As usual, however, Mother Jones was untroubled by the danger. "I'll come," she told the young miner. "I've been wanting to invade that place for quite a while."

Since the coal company owned twenty square miles of the Cabin Creek district, their guards could arrest as a trespasser anyone who came close to the mine. Mother Jones decided to hold her first labor rally in the village of Eksdale, several miles away. She gave the young man orders to hire a hall and print some handbills announcing the meeting for the day after tomorrow.

The following day, Ben Morris, a member of the United Mine Workers national board, took the train up from Charleston to Paint Creek to see Mother Jones. "I hear you're going to Cabin Creek tomorrow," he said. "Do you think that's wise?"

"It's not wise," she conceded, "but it's necessary."

"Well, if you insist on going," Morris said, "let me go with you."

"No," said Mother Jones. "It's better for me to go alone. You represent the national office, and if anything goes wrong, the operators will sue the union for damages. I'm a private citizen. All they can do is put me in jail. And I'm used to that."

Morris returned to Charleston and asked the Governor to send a company of militia up to Cabin Creek. Then he asked the local sheriff for a bodyguard and followed Mother Jones to Eksdale. The meeting was just getting started when Morris arrived. Out of deference to his position as a national board member, Mother Jones asked him to say a few words. Morris started talking to the men about patience and the need to trust in the justice of their cause.

Mother Jones leaped up, her white curls bouncing indignantly, "Stop that silly trash," she demanded.

The audience burst into applause. "Sit down! Sit down!" came the angry shouts. Ben Morris retreated to his chair, and Mary Harris Jones took over the rostrum.

"You men have come over the mountains," she said, "twelve, sixteen miles. Your clothes are thin. Your shoes are out at the toes. Your wives and little ones are cold and hungry! You have been robbed and enslaved for years! And now Billy Sunday comes to you and tells you to be good and patient and trust to justice! What silly trash to tell to men whose goodness and patience have cried out to a deaf world!"

A voice from the back of the hall rang out, "Organize us, Mother!" The demand quickly swelled to a roar. "Organize us! Organize us!"

Every man in the hall was begging to be sworn into the union. It was a dangerous decision. At Cabin Creek, a union member was liable to lose not only his job but his life. Mother Jones may have just reprimanded a member of the union's national board for talking mush, but she knew the union with its treasury and its years of strike experience was vital to any sustained resistance in Cabin Creek. "March over to the church on the corner," she told them. "It's dark enough there so you won't be seen."

Standing in the blackness on the church steps, the men raised their hands and pledged their loyalty to the union. "Now go home and keep your mouths shut," Mother Jones told them. "Don't say anything about being union men. Put on your overalls in the morning, take your dinner buckets, and go to work in the mines just as you've always done."

The men did as they were told, but when they arrived at the mines, they were all fired. Company spies had turned in a list of everyone who had attended the meeting. The workers retaliated by calling a strike that soon became as bitter and bloody as the one at Paint Creek.

Before Mother Jones left Eksdale, another group of miners arrived from Red Warrior Camp and asked her to speak to them. The men had brought a mule and buggy for transportation and a miner's son to serve as her driver. All the roads were company-owned, but they could drive along a shallow creek bed.

The miners returned to Red Warrior Camp with her. They traveled on foot, trudging along a railroad track that ran parallel to the creek but on a slight incline above it.

They had gone only a few miles when Mother Jones heard a shout from the railroad tracks. She looked up and saw the men darting along with their heads down, bullets whistling all around them. In two seconds, she was out of the buggy. "Stand where you are," she shouted. "I'm coming."

Clambering up the slope, she joined the miners, who by now were huddled together behind a large rock near a bend in the tracks. On the opposite side of the bend, a group of company guards manned a smoking machine gun.

"Keep back," the miners shouted to Mother Jones. "They'll kill you."

"I won't keep back," she snapped, "and no one is going to kill me."

Emerging from behind the rock, she walked straight up to the guards and placed the palm of her hand over the muzzle of their machine gun. "All right," she called to the miners. "You men can pass now."

The leader of the guards, a surly, unshaven man named Mayfield, glared at her ominously. "Take your hands off that gun, you hellcat," he growled.

Mother Jones didn't move. "Workers go into the mines out West to bring out the metal that makes this gun," she said. "Workers melt the minerals in furnaces and roll the steel. Workers dig the coal that feeds furnaces. We workers are not fighting you. We're fighting the men who rob us and deprive our children of childhood. It is the hard-earned pay of the working class that your pay comes from. They aren't fighting you."

Mayfield's confederates seemed ready to back down, but their leader was not so easily dissuaded. "I don't give a damn," he snarled. "I'm going to kill every one of these men and you, too."

Mother Jones looked at him coolly. "If you shoot one bullet out of this gun at those men," she said, "if you touch one of my white hairs, that creek will run with blood and yours will be the first to crimson it."

"Oh yeah?" sneered Mayfield. "And who's going to shoot me?"

Mother Jones pointed to the hills around them. "There are five hundred miners up there," she said. "And they all have guns. They're on their way to the same meeting I'm going to address. If they hear you shooting, they can be down here in five minutes."

Mayfield collapsed. "All right," he barked. "Go ahead."

Mother Jones stood there with her hand over the machine-gun muzzle until all the miners had made their way around the next bend in the tracks. Then she scrambled down to the creek bed, climbed back in her buggy, and went on to the meeting. There had been no armed men in the mountains, but the ruse had enabled her to save a few lives and organize still another local of the United Mine Workers.

Mary Harris Jones had made up her mind that she would not leave West Virginia until every mining district in the state had its own union local. One of the last places to be organized was Wineberg. Again the creek bed was the only public road, but this time it was early spring and the water was several feet deep. Mother Jones decided to walk along the railroad tracks. A few miles from the mining camp, she met her old friend Mayfield and his henchmen. They were armed with revolvers and had a machine gun set up along the tracks.

"You can't walk here," Mayfield said. "It's private property."

A reporter from the Baltimore *Sun* happened to be with Mother Jones. "You don't mean to say you're going to make an old lady walk in that ice-cold creek?" he asked.

Mayfield flashed him an evil grin. "It's too damn good for her," he muttered. "But don't worry, she won't walk it."

"Oh, won't I?" said Mother Jones. Taking off her high black shoes and stockings, she rolled up her skirts, stepped into the icy water, and waded up the creek to Wineberg.

When the waiting miners saw what she had done, they stepped into the water to meet her. With their overalls rolled up and their shoes in hand, they pledged their loyalty to the United Mine Workers Union.

Mother Jones finally brought the struggle between the miners and the West Virginia coal companies to a head in 1913. By now she was eighty-three. During an altercation at one of the mining districts, a company guard was killed, and she and several other labor organizers were jailed for conspiracy to commit murder. Her arrest focused national attention on the miners' problems. Her followers organized a protest meeting in Washington, D.C.; a sympathetic journalist, Mrs. Fremont Older, told the story of her exploits in *Collier's* magazine. In the ensuing furor, a Senate investigation was launched.

Pardoned by West Virginia's newly elected Governor, Mother Jones appeared before the committee and gave a detailed account of the misery she had seen at the mines. Thanks largely to her testimony, many abuses were corrected and the coal companies were forced to recognize their employees' right to join unions.

The victory in West Virginia was a major triumph for Mary Harris Jones. But that did not mean she forgot and forgave the abuses she had seen there. Like "Mamma" Truman, she was inclined to think that once a man revealed himself as a wrong'un, he would go on being one. She never let up on these characters until the day she died.

At the head of her list in West Virginia was a militia

general who had sided with the mine owners. He arrested strikers on the slightest pretext and further violated their civil rights by trying them in military courts without benefit of a jury.

While Mother Jones was in Washington testifying before the Senate Committee, the General sent a man to see her. To her astonishment, the emissary said that the General was running for Congress and hoped Mother Jones would write a letter endorsing him.

Mary Harris Jones's eighty-three-year-old eyes sparked. She had watched the General escort miners to the penitentiary after his court-martial board had given them ten- and fifteen-year sentences. She had listened to the sobs of their wives and children. She had seen the General give orders that the men were not permitted to kiss their families good-bye.

"Did the General send you?" she asked the already nervous messenger.

"Yes," was the reply.

"Tell him that nothing would give me more pleasure than to give him an endorsement. But it would be an endorsement to go to hell—not to Congress!"

The General did not get to Congress. But I wouldn't be surprised if the first half of Mother Jones's endorsement worked.

Part III

Three Faces
of Fortitude

Few contemporary books are complete without a sprinkling of four-letter words. This one is no exception—but the four-letter words that I'm going to use are not likely to offend even the most straight-laced reader. One is *guts*—the kind of stamina that enables people to "stomach" all kinds of disagreeable and frightening experiences. The other is a more old-fashioned but no less serviceable word—*grit*.

Of the two, guts is by far the more glamorous type of courage. It outwits enemies, refuses to be intimidated by mobs, is undaunted by bullets and bombs. Grit is less flamboyant. It is a steadfast determination to persist in spite of pain, misfortune, and bitter disappointment. The two-dollar word for it is fortitude.

I never had any doubt that fortitude was an admirable virtue, but it always used to strike me as rather dull. That was because I thought of it solely as patience in the face of difficulties that were beyond human control. In that context, it is passive rather than active and calls for forbearance rather than a fighting spirit. In the course of reading about women in American history, however, I have come to see that fortitude has another, much livelier, dimension.

Not all of the women who have persevered in the face of adversity were the victims of calamities beyond their control. Many went out of their way to choose their lot. They knew the choices would expose them to public scorn and private despair, but they made their decisions and they stuck to them.

I don't know whether fortitude comes more naturally to women than it does to men, but I'm inclined to believe that it does. I won't claim that all women are patient and persevering, but I think that most of us have learned not to expect instant results from our efforts. If we did, we'd never be able to put up with bearing and raising children. I think, too, that women, trained for years to take a back seat to men, find it easier to forgo public acclaim. They are quicker to see that virtue—particularly when the virtue is fortitude—has to be its own reward.

Like most people, I am dazzled by daring, but I also recognize the fact that it is easier to charge the heights of heroism in one brief, bold gesture than it is to struggle upward over the years. That is what fortitude is all about. It is a long-term, sometimes a lifetime, proposition. Worse yet, it is a gamble that may never pay off. Many women, and men too, never won the battles they embarked on; others did not live to see the final victories.

Fortitude is courage with faith but often without hope. It dreams of overcoming but is content merely to survive. I like the tough, hard sound of that four-letter word *grit,* but even when it hides behind its fancy label *fortitude,* its essence remains the same. It's a brand of courage that demands exceptional strength of mind and spirit, and I can't help cheering the women who rose to its challenge.

Trust a Woman As a Doctor— *Never!*

When I first decided to embark on a career as a professional singer, there were more than a few raised eyebrows around the country. The idea of a President's daughter pursuing such a goal was not only unheard of but unthinkable. No matter that I had always had a strong interest in music. No matter that several highly reputable experts thought that I had talent. The daughter of the President of the United States had no business trying to support herself as a performer.

Happily, there were many more people, including my parents, who saw no reason why I shouldn't chart my life in whatever direction I pleased. But my own brief skirmish with the arbiters of what someone should, or should not do, has made me peculiarly sensitive to the problems of any woman who elects to disturb the status quo.

I began my singing career in 1947—a comparatively enlightened era—and I was going into a field where women were not only welcomed but acclaimed. I have often wondered if I would have had the courage to stick to my guns in a less liberated age or a more male-dominated profession. Could I, for instance, have endured the loneliness and discouragement that Elizabeth Blackwell had to put up with in her struggle to become America's first woman doctor? I doubt it very much. She was tackling a field where women were not only unheard of but very definitely unwanted. And she was doing it at a time when respectable young women were supposed to do little more than look pretty and make good marriages.

Elizabeth Blackwell launched her career in 1847. The differences in the worlds we lived in are staggering. The women of her era were shielded from everything—higher education, exercise, even the facts of life. Business and the professions were barred to them. They were not allowed to serve on juries, testify in court, or cast their ballots in an election.

To make matters worse, the men and women of the Victorian era suffered from an exaggerated sense of propriety, particularly about anything concerning the human body. Legs, if they were referred to at all, became limbs, and nude paintings and sculpture, including some of the world's greatest masterpieces, were considered only just this side of pornography. In an atmosphere like that, you can imagine the courage it took for a young, unmarried woman to apply for admission to medical school.

Of course, anyone who knew anything about Elizabeth Blackwell's childhood might have predicted that she would turn out to be a courageous young woman. Born near Bristol, England, in 1821, she was the oldest daughter of two courageous parents, Samuel and Hannah Lane Blackwell.

Samuel Blackwell owned a successful sugar refinery, but his interests went far beyond those of the average businessman. An intelligent and warmhearted man, he was an enthusiastic supporter of such reforms as religious tolerance, women's rights, and the abolition of slavery. Nor was Han-

CULVER PICTURES INC.

Apparently no picture of the young Elizabeth Blackwell has survived. But this portrait, painted in her later years, gives us a good look at the courage that made her America's first woman doctor.

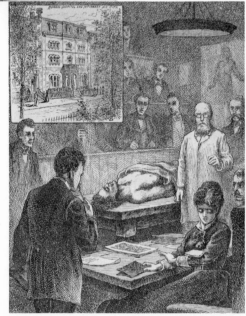

CULVER PICTURES INC.

This print shows Dr. Blackwell at work in the operating room. She wanted to become a surgeon. But an eye injury made this an impossibility. The New York Infirmary for Women and Children is in the upper left-hand corner.

nah Blackwell simply a docile helpmate to her energetic husband. She had a pleasant personality of her own and, in addition to raising a large family, saw to it that they shared her enthusiasm for music and reading.

Between Hannah Blackwell's hospitable nature and her husband's stimulating conversation, the Blackwell home became a magnet for some of the leading intellectuals of the period. Thus, from her earliest years, Elizabeth was exposed to people who valued clear thinking, social awareness, and new ideas.

Samuel Blackwell was a deeply religious man, but he was a Dissenter—one who refused to follow the teaching of the Church of England. Many earlier groups of Dissenters, beginning with the Pilgrims, had found religious asylum in America. By the early nineteenth century, some of the dis-crimination against Dissenters had abated, but they were still subject to certain strictures. One was that their children could not attend publicly supported schools.

Fortunately, Samuel Blackwell had enough money to hire private tutors for his children. As a result, the youngsters not only received a better education than they would have gotten in a regular school but, in accordance with the elder Blackwell's decree, the girls were allowed to pursue the same course of study as the boys.

With this kind of background, it isn't too surprising that the nine Blackwell children grew up with none of the usual nineteenth-century notions about inequality between the sexes. Five of the girls had careers. Elizabeth and Emily became doctors, Anna was a newspaper correspondent, Marian a teacher, and Ellen an author and artist. One brother, Samuel, married Antoinette Brown, America's first woman minister. Another, Henry, married Lucy Stone, the woman's rights leader who steadfastly refused to be called by her husband's name.

Between 1830 and 1832, England was in the throes of so much political and social unrest that many people thought the country was on the brink of a revolution. Samuel Blackwell had been toying with the idea of emigrating to the United States. When his sugar refinery was destroyed by a fire in 1832, he finally made up his mind.

The Blackwells settled first in New York and later in Cincinnati. But the success that so many other men had found in the New World eluded Samuel Blackwell. For one thing, his views on Abolition made him unpopular with his associates in the sugar-refining business. In that era, sugar was produced almost exclusively by slave labor. Then, the panic of 1837 dealt him a severe financial blow. A year later, Samuel Blackwell died, leaving his widow and children practically destitute.

To support the family, Hannah Blackwell and her three oldest daughters, Elizabeth, Anna, and Marian, opened a private school. Elizabeth spent four years teaching there and another year working at a school in Henderson, Kentucky. After five years in the classroom, she decided that her one ambition in life was to become a doctor.

I've often wondered what possessed Elizabeth Blackwell to choose such a difficult path. She lacked the fire and rage of the typical iconoclast. Moreover, by her own admission, she had never had any great interest in the human body and its various ailments. But teaching did not offer her the kind of intellectual stimulation she needed, and although she liked men and had several eligible suitors, the prospect of marriage—the usual alternative for a woman of her era—made her apprehensive.

It's not hard to see why. Elizabeth Blackwell was intelligent and self-reliant. Nineteenth-century marriage seemed designed to stifle both qualities. Wives were not encouraged to have any interests outside of the home. They were expected to defer to their husbands in public and often in private as well. They were also barred from owning property, signing legal documents, and managing their own affairs. They became, as the suffragists phrased it, "civilly dead." It was not an appealing prospect for a woman like Elizabeth Blackwell. A career in medicine, no matter how difficult, seemed like a far more attractive choice.

Deciding on a medical career took guts. Trying to launch one demanded grit. Elizabeth wrote to a long list of schools—Harvard, Yale, Bowdoin, several in New York, several more in Philadelphia—and was rejected by every one. Then she tried the small and not particularly prestigious Geneva Medical College in upstate New York. Much to her surprise, a letter of acceptance came back. It wasn't until she arrived on the campus that she found out why.

The dean, reluctant to take the responsibility for admitting a woman, had put her application to a vote of the school. The students, a bunch of boisterous farmboys, thought the letter was a practical joke being played by a rival college and amidst a chorus of cheers and catcalls, voted to accept her.

Elizabeth Blackwell made few friends during the two years she spent at the Geneva Medical College. The townspeople were convinced that any woman who studied anatomy was immoral. Her fellow students were more broad-minded, but they nevertheless regarded her as a curiosity. For Elizabeth, it was a long and lonely experience, but in the course of it she developed a true fascination for medicine. A medical degree became no longer just an escape from marriage; it was the passport to a lifetime of excitement and service.

Then, as now, medical school training had to be supplemented with practical experience. Elizabeth elected to take her internship in Europe, where the hospitals were better and the prejudice against women was not as strong.

Her decision was a sound one, but, unfortunately, another pitfall awaited her. While working at La Maternité Hospital in Paris, she treated a child suffering from a highly contagious eye disease and contracted the condition herself. She lost the sight of one eye and was forced to abandon the medical specialty she had set her heart on pursuing—surgery.

It took a long while to recover from both the illness and the disappointment, but eventually Elizabeth completed her internship and was ready to think about setting up a practice. A small but prestigious group of Londoners, impressed by her medical skill and her pioneering spirit, urged her to stay in England. But Elizabeth had made up her mind to return to the United States. She knew that the prejudice against women was strong in both countries, but she was convinced that America was the place where they would finally be recognized as "the equal half of humanity." Before too long, Elizabeth Blackwell had good reason to wonder if her confidence in her country had been misplaced.

Arriving in New York in the summer of 1851, Elizabeth began looking for a place to open her first office. She was thirty years old, a slender five-foot-two-inch blonde with a plain but not unpleasant face. She was well educated and respectable, but when she tried to rent rooms, she might as well have been a common prostitute. The minute she mentioned that she was a doctor, she was treated to a scorching tirade. The script became painfully familiar. A doctor! No decent woman called herself a doctor. She must be involved in something disreputable. Probably an abortionist like that dreadful Madame Restell who lived in a mansion on Fifth Avenue and whose "midwifery" practice was the talk of New York. After a while, Elizabeth began to think she was lucky when all she got was a door slammed in her face.

After weeks of trudging the streets searching for To Let signs, she finally found rooms in a house near Washington Square. The landlady evinced no interest in what she planned to do with them, and Elizabeth made no effort to tell her. A week later a notice appeared in the New York *Tribune*:

> Miss Elizabeth Blackwell, M.D., has returned to this city from a two years' residence abroad, which she spent at the hospital of La Maternité in Paris and at St. Bartholomew's in London. She has just opened an office at Number 44, University Place, and is prepared to practice in every department of her profession.

The announcement might as well have never appeared. Not a single patient showed up. Day after day, Elizabeth found herself staring at the walls of her deserted office. To make matters worse, the members of her own profession were just as suspicious as everyone else.

Soon after she arrived in New York, she had applied to a leading hospital for permission to work as an assistant in their department for women and children. The reply was a prompt and unqualified no. Next she tried the municipal hospital, but again the answer was no. This time they did not even put it in writing. They just never answered her letter.

On top of these disappointments, she had to contend with a steady stream of hate mail. Along with the usual comparisons to Mme. Restell, there were remarks about her personal morality and even a few threats and some warnings to get out of town.

Elizabeth ignored the letters. She had too many other problems to worry about. With every opportunity to practice her profession barred to her, she was desperate for a way to support herself. Almost as desperate was the need to fill her long patientless days. She solved both problems by preparing a series of lectures on the physical education of girls. When they were finished, she rented the basement of a downtown church and advertised the series in *The New York Times.*

To Elizabeth's amazement, practically every seat in the room was filled. It was the audience's turn to be amazed when Dr. Blackwell began expounding her ideas about bringing up girls. She recommended getting out in the fresh air and sunshine and engaging in such physical activities as climbing, wrestling, and running. She also described the process of childbirth, advocated sex education, and insisted that women could, and should, take a more active role in society.

Several of the women who attended the lectures were scandalized by Elizabeth Blackwell's radical theories, but luckily there were also a large number of Quakers in the audience. Always receptive to ideas that furthered the goal of equal rights, the Quaker women gave Elizabeth Blackwell their wholehearted support.

As a result of the lecture series, she secured a new lease on her faltering medical career. Several of the women engaged her as their physician, and one, the wife of a successful printer, insisted that she deliver her first grandchild.

Although she now had about a dozen patients, Elizabeth was still far from being accepted on an equal basis with the other members of her profession. Once, when she was treating an elderly woman who had pneumonia, she called in another doctor, an old friend of her father's, for consultation. The man examined the patient and returned to the parlor. "A most extraordinary case!" he exclaimed, wringing his hands and pacing up and down the room. "Nothing like this has ever happened to me before. I really don't know what to do."

At first, Elizabeth was confused. The patient obviously had pneumonia, and there were no serious complications. She had only called in the second doctor as a precaution. Then it suddenly dawned on her that the man wasn't upset about her patient at all. He was worried about the propriety of holding a consultation with a woman doctor.

The man was such a close friend that Elizabeth found it hard to be angry with him. She simply sighed and said gently, "If it makes you uneasy, please don't consider this a medical consultation. Just look on it as a talk between two old friends."

The doctor looked vastly relieved. He confirmed Elizabeth's diagnosis, recommended a treatment, and the patient recovered. Thereafter, whenever Elizabeth wanted his advice, she simply invited him around for a "friendly talk."

Elizabeth's old friend was more tolerant than a lot of other New Yorkers. Dr. Blackwell was still regarded in most circles as either a freak or a fallen woman. People stared at her on the street and pointed her out to their friends. A few women crossed the street to avoid her, others held onto their skirts lest they brush against hers when they passed. She became known around town as "that weird little doctress." She could tolerate being called "weird" and "little," but she hated the term doctress with its implication that she was somehow inferior to a male doctor.

Even worse than the scorn and ridicule was the loneliness. Elizabeth had no close friends, no one to talk to or visit with, no one with whom to share a meal or an evening off. "I understand now why this life has never been lived before," she wrote to one of her sisters. "It is hard, with no support but a high purpose, to live against every species of social opposition. I should like a little fun now and then. Life is altogether too sober."

At the beginning of 1853, Elizabeth Blackwell had been in New York for a year and a half. The Quakers who had originally supported her continued to do so, but her practice was still woefully small. Sometimes, she saw only three patients a week. She had tried again and again to find a place on a hospital staff, but her efforts constantly met with rebuffs. The directors of the municipal dispensary told her she "would not promote the harmonious working of the institution" and suggested that if she wanted to work in a dispensary, she should start one of her own.

A year earlier, the advice would have been ridiculous, but now Elizabeth was not so sure. Her Quaker friends had already offered her their financial support. In addition, her younger sister Emily had enrolled at the Rush Medical School in Chicago and would eventually be joining her in New York. With another doctor to help her, Elizabeth felt confident she could manage her own dispensary.

Elizabeth rented a tiny room in a house on East Seventh Street just off Tompkins Square. The neighborhood, one of New York's worst slums, was a clutter of filthy, rat-infested tenements. Babies were born, and often died, in their dark airless rooms. Their mothers fared no better. There was rarely a doctor or even a midwife in attendance, and minor complications often proved fatal.

Ignorance and poverty also took their toll. Nutrition and cleanliness were unknown, and mothers and children seldom went out in the fresh air. The poor families around Tompkins Square were desperately in need of medical care, but they were as leery of a woman doctor as the well-to-do families around Washington Square.

The clinic opened in March, 1853. Elizabeth hung a sign outside, announcing that it would be open three afternoons a week and that all patients would be treated free. For the first few weeks, no one showed up. Then, one day, a woman staggered up the stone steps and collapsed in Elizabeth's arms. She was in such agony that she did not care who treated her. The woman had a serious but not incurable infection of the uterus. She was treated kindly, and when she recovered, began telling all her friends about the wonderful doctor on Seventh Street.

The dispensary was soon going well, and before long Elizabeth's private practice also began to improve. It was not unusual for her to be called out at midnight to see a sick woman in Flushing or deliver a baby in Flatbush. She tried to look purposeful and businesslike when she walked the shadowy streets or boarded the empty horsecars, but she was often approached by drunks and strangers who mistook her for a prostitute.

Her mysterious comings and goings and the strange hours she kept soon aroused the suspicions of her landlady. Convinced that she was performing secret abortions, the woman began hiding her mail and stopping patients at the front door to tell them Dr. Blackwell was not at home.

The situation finally got so bad that Elizabeth had to move. Her Quaker friends again came to her rescue and loaned her enough money for a down payment on a house on East Fifteenth Street. The upper floors had to be rented to pay off the mortgage, but there was a large consulting room on the first floor, and Elizabeth's own parlor was converted into a waiting room.

By now the Tompkins Square dispensary was going so well that Elizabeth Blackwell was dreaming bigger dreams. She wanted to expand the one-room clinic into a full-fledged hospital and eventually add a nurses' training school and a women's medical college as well. Her Quaker supporters volunteered to help with the fund-raising, and Elizabeth began looking for a building to house the fledgling hospital. She found an old Dutch house on Bleecker Street not far from Tompkins Square, on the edge of another slum called the Five Points. The building had to be completely renovated. Walls were ripped down; one bedroom became an operating room, another a delivery room. The parlor floor was transformed into a ward.

Chartered as the New York Infirmary for Women and Children, the new hospital was dedicated on May 12, 1857. Its establishment was a historic first—a hospital for women staffed by women.

It had taken six long years for the barriers of prejudice to begin to crumble. During that time, Elizabeth Blackwell proved to the New York medical community that she was both competent and dedicated. Several leading male doctors agreed to serve as consulting physicians at the new hospital. Meanwhile, her Quaker admirers had been telling the city's more broad-minded laymen about her work. The editor of the New York *Tribune,* Horace Greeley, and the founder of *The New York Times,* Henry J. Raymond, accepted Dr. Blackwell's invitation to join the New York Infirmary's board of trustees, and the women doctors soon had the wholehearted support of their editorial pages.

But Elizabeth Blackwell's struggle to be accepted as a fully qualified and respectable member of her profession was by no means over. One day when she was trying to figure out a way to raise money for her new hospital, she recalled that the English actress Fanny Kemble sometimes gave readings from Shakespeare for the benefit of worthy causes. Elizabeth had met the actress in London and had found her a gracious and pleasant person. When she arrived in New York for an American tour, she went to call on her.

Fanny Kemble remembered their previous meeting. She greeted Elizabeth cordially and was interested to learn that she was there on behalf of the New York Infirmary. "It sounds like a good cause," she said. "Tell me more about it."

Elizabeth began describing the hospital and its patients. She explained that many of them were receiving decent medical care for the first time in their lives. They paid practically nothing for it. The standard fee was four dollars a week; those who couldn't afford it were treated free.

Fanny Kemble nodded enthusiastically until Elizabeth began discussing the doctors at the hospital. When the actress realized that the New York Infirmary was staffed entirely by women, her expressive eyes registered horror. She leaped to her feet, waved her slender hands dramatically, and exclaimed, "Trust a woman as a doctor . . . *Never!*"

It was a shock for Elizabeth to discover that when it came to women doctors, even a successful and sophisticated woman could be as narrow and prim as the most sheltered housewife.

The man in the street displayed a more violent kind of prejudice. One of the first patients at the hospital, a woman in labor, subsequently died of puerperal fever. Within an hour a large crowd had gathered on Bleecker Street. The leaders pounded on the hospital door with their fists and demanded that the lady doctors stop killing innocent women.

Elizabeth Blackwell, peering out of an upstairs window, was shaken by the mob's fury. The men were armed with pickaxes and shovels. They shouted angrily and brandished their tools like weapons. Taking a deep breath and steeling herself for the confrontation, Elizabeth went downstairs to meet them. The instant she appeared on the front steps, the mob let out a howl of rage. Elizabeth felt a tremor of fear run through her body. She fully expected that in another minute her hospital would be wrecked and she and her staff beaten or killed.

Suddenly, a brawny man in overalls pushed his way to the front of the crowd. His face was smeared with dirt, and he too had a shovel slung over his shoulder. Elizabeth recognized him as a member of a construction gang that was laying a water main in the next block.

The man leaped up on the steps and in a thick Irish brogue ordered the mob to be quiet. "These doctors took good care of my wife and children," he told them. "They're fine ladies and they do the best they can."

Amazingly, the clamor subsided, and the crowd drifted back to their homes.

On another occasion, a woman with a ruptured appendix was admitted to the Infirmary. When she died a few hours later, another mob appeared on Bleecker Street. This time they threw rocks at the windows, shouting, "Quacks! Quacks! Women quacks!"

Elizabeth was deeply troubled by the woman's death. She was disturbed, too, to discover that she was being held responsible for it. The charge was totally unjust. Moreover, it would damage her reputation as a doctor and cast doubt on the ability of any woman who elected to practice medicine.

Elizabeth Blackwell knew that she had to stand up to her accusers. She sent a hasty message to the city coroner and asked him to come around at once and perform an autopsy on the dead woman. The mob was still milling outside the Infirmary when he arrived. Without a second's thought for her own safety, Elizabeth stepped outside and calmly asked for twelve volunteers to come in and act as witnesses.

Elizabeth Blackwell stayed in the room while the autopsy was performed. The coroner completed his job and concluded that without question, the woman's death had been inevitable. The twelve witnesses looked so embarrassed that Elizabeth actually felt sorry for them. "I understand how you feel," she said sympathetically, "but I hope you'll understand how we feel, too. We women doctors, after all, have to prove ourselves."

Dr. Blackwell and her associates did prove themselves. The New York Infirmary grew into a large and thriving hospital which today occupies a modern skyscraper on East Fifteenth Street. It was a long time before the prejudice against women doctors diminished, but thanks to Elizabeth Blackwell's fortitude, medical schools and hospital staffs now admit women along with men and most people recognize the fact that doctors' abilities are measured by skill and training, not by their sex.

The United States
vs. *Susan B. Anthony*

Susan B. Anthony has never been one of my favorite characters. Stern-eyed and grim-lipped, she seemed utterly devoid
of warmth and humor and much too quick to dominate the
women she worked with. I always thought her personality
could be summed up in one word: battle-ax. On top of that
drawback, she was a fanatic. She joined the woman's suffrage
movement in 1852, when she was thirty-two years old. From
then until her death in 1906, she could think of little else.

The fanatics of one generation have a habit of turning into the heroes and heroines of the next, as Susan B.
Anthony proved. And since I've been making a study of
heroines, I decided to give Miss Anthony a second look. I
have to report that my original assessment of her character
was much too harsh.

Susan B. Anthony came to the woman's movement
by a somewhat circuitous route. She was a reformer by in-
heritance as well as by temperament. Her parents were passionate supporters of abolition, temperance, and woman's
rights. They numbered among their friends some of the outstanding liberals of the nineteenth century, men like William
Lloyd Garrison, Frederick Douglass, and Prudence Crandall's
old ally, the Reverend Samuel J. May.

Daniel Anthony had a succession of homes, a succession of jobs, and a succession of financial ups and downs. He began his career as a farmer in Adams, Massachusetts, but gave up farming to buy a cotton mill near Albany, New York. His business was wrecked by the panic of 1837, and he bought another farm, this one a small plot of land just outside of Rochester, New York.

The collapse of the cotton mill left the Anthony family with a mountain of debts. Susan, by then in her late teens, became a teacher to help pay them off. After ten years in the classroom, she resigned and took over the management of her father's farm so Daniel Anthony could devote his attention to still another business venture—an insurance agency that eventually made him prosperous once more.

As I mentioned earlier, the instinct for reform had been bred into Susan since childhood. She was particularly concerned about temperance, and her work in that movement soon brought her in contact with Amelia Bloomer, who ran a temperance newspaper in Seneca Falls. Mrs. Bloomer introduced her to another temperance advocate, Elizabeth Cady Stanton, who was now pouring most of her energies into a campaign to give women the vote. Mrs. Stanton tried to enlist Susan's support in the suffrage movement, but Susan demurred. She was too busy with temperance activities to have time for anything else.

In 1852, Susan B. Anthony attended a rally in Albany where she was refused permission to speak because of her sex. The incident made her so angry that she withdrew from the regular temperance organization and set up a separate Woman's New York State Temperance Society with Elizabeth Cady Stanton as its president.

Not long after that, Susan went to a convention of the New York State Teachers' Association. More than two-thirds of the members were women, but the men ran the entire

THE BETTMANN
ARCHIVE INC.

Susan B. Anthony was not beautiful, but she was also not the ugly bitter old maid that her enemies said she was. This was how she looked around the time she defied a corrupt judge and risked a prison sentence for her cause.

THE BETTMANN
ARCHIVE INC.

This print is a good example of the abuse Susan B. Anthony endured during her long struggle to win the vote for women.

meeting, giving the speeches, voting on resolutions, and generally ignoring the women, who sat in an isolated bloc at the back of the room.

When a panel of male speakers began a lengthy debate on the topic: "Why the profession of a teacher is not as much respected as that of lawyer, doctor, or minister," Susan requested permission to state her opinion on the matter. After some discussion, the men agreed to let her be heard.

Susan offered a very simple answer to the question. "Do you not see," she said, "that so long as society says woman is incompetent to be a lawyer, minister, or doctor, but has ample ability to be a teacher, every man of you who chooses this profession tacitly acknowledges that he has no more brains than a woman?"

She went on to say a few words about the disparity in the salaries of men and women teachers. It would be to the men's advantage to equalize them, she maintained, because their own incomes suffered when they had to compete with the cheap labor of women.

The speech left most of Susan's audience in a state of shock. A few men rushed over to congratulate her; the women remained silent. But she made at least one convert. A woman from Rochester pushed through a resolution affirming the right of women teachers to participate in all of the association's activities, including speaking at meetings, serving on committees, and holding office.

Susan B. Anthony's success with the teachers' association convinced her that discrimination against women should —and could—be overcome. Before long, she had become Elizabeth Cady Stanton's chief lieutenant in the woman's rights movement. Mrs. Stanton had young children at the time and was not free to travel extensively. She concentrated on writing letters and speeches, while Susan did most of the legwork. She proved to be a brilliant organizer and an indefatigable lecturer, a master at circulating petitions, organizing conventions, and browbeating politicians.

All of the women who had the guts to demand the right to vote were cruelly criticized in the press, but Susan was invariably singled out as a special target. The fact that she was unmarried made her particularly vulnerable. This was declared proof positive that her crusade was simply the ranting of an embittered old maid.

The insulting newspaper articles and vicious cartoons must have bothered Susan. But she never let it show. She threw herself into her work. There was always a new speech to write, a new meeting to organize, a new petition to be drawn up and presented to a state legislature.

Susan B. Anthony was a stern and single-minded woman. Like most crusaders for causes—especially unpopular causes—she had little time for fun and games. But I have a sneaky feeling that behind her severe manner and unremitting devotion to duty, she may actually have had a sense of humor. Let me tell you about my favorite episode in Susan B. Anthony's career, and perhaps you'll agree.

It began on Friday morning, November 1, 1872. Susan was reading the morning paper at her home in Rochester. There, at the top of the editorial page of the *Democrat and Chronicle,* was an exhortation to the city's residents:

> Now register! Today and tomorrow are the only remaining opportunities. If you were not permitted to vote, you would fight for the right, undergo all privations for it, face death for it. You have it now at the cost of five minutes' time to be spent in seeking your place of registration and having your name entered. And yet, on election day, less than a week hence, hundreds of you are likely to

lose your votes because you have not thought it worth while to give the five minutes. Today and tomorrow are your only opportunities. Register now!

Susan B. Anthony read the editorial again. Just as she thought, it said nothing about being addressed to men only. With a gleam in her eye, she put down the paper and summoned her sister Guelma, with whom she lived. The two women donned their hats and cloaks and went off to call on two other Anthony sisters who lived nearby. Together, the four women headed for the barber shop on West Street, where voters from the Eighth Ward were being registered.

For some time, Susan B. Anthony had been looking for an opportunity to test the Fourteenth Amendment to the Constitution as a weapon to win the vote for women. Adopted in 1870, the Amendment had been designed to protect the civil rights—especially the voting rights—of recently freed slaves. It stated that:

> All persons born or naturalized in the United States, and subject to the jurisdiction thereof, are citizens of the United States and of the State wherein they reside. No State shall make or enforce any law which shall abridge the privileges or immunities of citizens of the United States, nor shall any State deprive any person of life, liberty, or property without due process of law, nor deny to any person within its jurisdiction the equal protection of the laws.

The Amendment did not say that "persons" meant only males, nor did it spell out "the privileges and immunities of citizens." Susan B. Anthony felt perfectly justified in concluding that the right to vote was among the privileges of citizenship and that it extended to women as well as men. I'm sure she must have also seen the humor of outwitting the supposedly superior males who wrote the Amendment.

It was bad enough for a bunch of women to barge

into one sacred male precinct—the barber shop—but to insist on being admitted to another holy of holies—the voting booth—was absolutely outrageous. Moustaches twitched, throats were cleared, a whispered conference was held in the corner.

Susan had brought along a copy of the Fourteenth Amendment. She read it aloud, carefully pointing out to the men in charge of registration that the document failed to state that the privilege of voting extended only to males.

Only one man in the barber shop had the nerve to refuse the Anthony sisters the right to register. The rest buckled under Susan's determined oratory and allowed them to sign the huge, leather-bound voter registration book. If the men in the barber shop thought they were getting rid of a little band of crackpots the easy way, they were wrong. Susan urged all her followers in Rochester to register. The next day, a dozen women invaded the Eighth Ward barber shop, and another thirty-five appeared at registration sites elsewhere in the city. The *Democrat and Chronicle,* which had inadvertently prompted the registrations, expressed no editorial opinion on the phenomenon, but its rival, the *Union and Advertiser,* denounced the women. If they were allowed to vote, the paper declared, the poll inspectors "should be prosecuted to the full extent of the law."

The following Tuesday, November 5, was Election Day. Most of the poll inspectors in Rochester had read the editorial in the *Union and Advertiser* and were too intimidated to allow any of the women who had registered to vote. Only in the Eighth Ward did the males weaken. Maybe the inspectors were *Democrat and Chronicle* readers, or perhaps they were more afraid of Susan B. Anthony than they were of the law. Whatever the reason, when Susan and her sisters showed up at the polls shortly after 7 A.M., there was only a minimum of fuss. A couple of inspectors were hesitant about letting the women vote, but when Susan assured them that she would pay all their legal expenses if they were prosecuted, the men relented, and one by one, the women took their ballots and stepped into the voting booth. There were no insults or sneers, no rude remarks. They marked their ballots, dropped them into the ballot box, and returned to their homes.

Susan B. Anthony's feat quickly became the talk of the country. She was applauded in some circles, vilified in others. But the day of reckoning was not long in arriving. On November 28, Deputy U. S. Marshal E. J. Keeney appeared at her door with a warrant for her arrest. She had violated Section 19 of the Enforcement Act of the Fourteenth Amendment, which held that anyone who voted illegally was to be arrested and tried on criminal charges.

Susan B. Anthony was a great believer in planning ahead. The day after she registered, she decided to get a legal opinion on whether or not she should attempt to vote. A number of lawyers turned her away, but she finally found one who agreed to consider the case. He was Henry R. Selden, a former judge of the Court of Appeals, now a partner in one of Rochester's most prestigious law firms.

On the Monday before Election Day, Henry Selden informed his new client that he agreed with her interpretation of the Fourteenth Amendment and that in his opinion, she had every right to cast her ballot. The U. S. Commissioner of Elections in Rochester, William C. Storrs, did not concur.

E. J. Keeney, the marshal dispatched to arrest Susan B. Anthony, was not at all happy with his assignment. He nervously twirled his tall felt hat while waiting for her to come to the front door. When she finally appeared, he blushed and stammered, shifted uncomfortably from one foot to the other, and finally blurted out, "The Commissioner wishes to arrest you."

Susan couldn't help being amused at Keeney's embarrassment. "Is this your usual method of serving a warrant?" she asked calmly. With that, the marshal recovered his official dignity, presented her with the warrant, and told her that he had come to escort her to the office of the Commissioner of Elections.

When Susan asked if she could change into a more suitable dress, the marshal saw his opportunity to escape. "Of course," he said, turning to leave. "Just come down to the Commissioner's office whenever you're ready."

"I'll do no such thing," Susan informed him curtly. "You were sent here to arrest me and take me to court. It's your duty to do so."

Keeney had no choice but to wait while his prisoner went upstairs and put on a more appropriate outfit. When she returned, she thrust out her wrists and said, "Don't you want to handcuff me, too?"

"I assure you, madam," Marshal Keeney stuttered, "it isn't at all necessary."

With the U. S. Marshal at her side, Susan was brought before the Federal Commissioner of Elections, William C. Storrs. Her arrest was recorded, and she was ordered to appear the next day for a hearing. It was conducted by U. S. District Attorney Richard Crowley and his assistant, John E. Pound.

Susan answered District Attorney Crowley's questions politely. She said that she thought the Fourteenth Amendment gave her the right to vote. She admitted that she had consulted an attorney on the question but said that she would have voted even if he had not advised her to do so. When Crowley asked if she had voted deliberately to test the law, she said, "Yes, sir. I have been determined for three years to vote the first time I happened to be at home for the required thirty days before an election."

The District Attorney's next step was to convene a grand jury to draw up a bill of indictment. He and his assistant fell to wrangling over a suitable trial date. Susan interrupted them. "I have lecture dates that will take me to central Ohio," she said. "I won't be available until December 10."

"But you're supposed to be in custody until the hearing," Crowley informed her.

"Is that so?" said Susan coolly. "I didn't know that."

The District Attorney backed down without an argument and scheduled the grand jury session for December 23.

Sixteen women had voted in Rochester. All sixteen were arrested and taken before the grand jury, but Susan alone was brought to trial. The District Attorney had decided to single her out as a test case. The three poll inspectors who had allowed the women to vote were also arrested. The grand jury indicted them too, set bail at five hundred dollars each, and ordered their trial set for the summer term of the U. S. District Court.

Susan Anthony's case now involved nineteen other men and woman. All of them—including Susan—were liable to go to prison if they were found guilty and the judge was in a sentencing mood. Prison in the 1870s was a very unpleasant place. There were no minimum security setups where a benevolent government allowed corrupt politicians, crooked labor leaders, and political agitators to rest and rehabilitate, as we do today. Prison meant a cold cell, wretched food, the company of thieves and murderers.

For a while it looked as if Susan might be behind bars even before her trial. She refused to post a bond for her five-hundred-dollar bail. Henry Selden paid the money for her. "I could not see a lady I respected put in jail," he said.

It must be agonizing to sweat out the weeks before a trial. There is time to look ahead and brood about the possibility of an unfavorable verdict and time to look back, perhaps with regret, at the decision that placed you in the hands of the law. But Susan B. Anthony had no regrets. Nor did she appear to have any anxieties about her trial. She had already proven her fortitude by devoting twenty years of her life to fighting for the right to vote. If she won her case, the struggle would be over. But even if she lost, Susan was not ready to give up the fight.

Some prospective defendants are too demoralized to do anything but sit around and worry. Not Susan B. Anthony. In the course of the next few months, she attended woman's rights conventions in Ohio, Illinois, and Indiana. She appeared before a session that was meeting in Albany to revise the New York State Constitution and tried to persuade them to include equal suffrage among its provisions. Then she went back to Rochester to cast her ballot again in the city elections on March 4, 1873.

Deputy Marshal Keeney appeared at the railroad every time she left Rochester. He reminded her that she was not supposed to leave the city while she was out on bail. Susan would smile, nod, and get on the train. Keeney never tried to stop her.

The summer term of the District Court opened in May. In mid-March, Susan launched a new lecture tour. Her topic: Is it a crime for a citizen of the United States to vote? The lecture centered on the U. S. Constitution, particularly the Fourteenth Amendment.

She spoke in every town in New York's Monroe County and drew surprisingly large audiences. When she polled the crowd at the end of each lecture, the majority invariably supported her. Even those who had been skeptics when they entered the hall usually changed their minds when they heard her arguments.

District Attorney Crowley soon decided that Susan was making it difficult for him to find an unprejudiced jury anywhere in the vicinity of Rochester. When he voiced his concern to Susan, she replied by asking him if he honestly believed that a jury could be prejudiced by having the Constitution of the United States read and explained to them.

Crowley became so exasperated that when the District Court opened on May 13, he requested a change of venue from Rochester to Canandaigua in adjacent Ontario County. The change forced a postponement of the trial until June 17. Susan promptly launched a whirlwind lecture tour of the villages around Canandaigua. She managed to cover twenty-one postal districts on her own, while her good friend and supporter, Matilda Joslyn Gage, covered the remaining sixteen.

The trial of *The United States* vs. *Susan B. Anthony* opened on the afternoon of June 17, 1873, with the tolling of the Canandaigua Courthouse bell. The presiding justice was Ward Hunt, a prim, pale man, who owed his judgeship to the good offices of Senator Roscoe Conkling, the Republican boss of New York State. Conkling was a fierce foe of woman suffrage, and Hunt, who had no wish to offend his powerful patron, had written his decision before the trial started.

District Attorney Crowley opened the arguments for the prosecution. They didn't make much sense at the time, and in retrospect, they sound nothing short of ridiculous. The District Attorney mentioned that Susan B. Anthony was a woman and therefore she had no right to vote. His principal witness was an inspector of elections for the Eighth Ward, who swore that on November 5 he had seen Miss Anthony put her ballot in the ballot box. To back up his testimony, the inspector produced the voter registration book with Susan B. Anthony's signature in it.

Henry Selden's reply for the defense was equally simple. He contended that Susan Anthony had registered and voted in good faith, believing that it was her constitutional right to do so. When he attempted to call his client to the stand, however, District Attorney Crowley announced that she was not competent to testify in her own behalf. Judge Hunt agreed, and the only thing Henry Selden could do was read excerpts from the testimony Susan had given at her previous hearings when presumably she was no less incompetent than she was right now.

Henry Selden tried to make up for this gross injustice by making his closing argument a dramatic, three-hour speech on behalf of woman suffrage. District Attorney Crowley replied with a two-hour rehash of the original charge.

By the afternoon of June 18, the case of *The United States* vs. *Susan B. Anthony* was ready to go to the jury. It was impossible to predict what their verdict might be, so Judge Hunt, determined to make it the verdict he and Roscoe Conkling wanted, took matters into his own hands. "Gentlemen of the jury," he said, "I direct that you find the defendant guilty."

Henry Selden leaped to his feet. "I object, your honor," he thundered. "The court has no power to direct the jury in a criminal case."

Judge Hunt ignored him. "Take the verdict, Mr. Clerk," he said.

The clerk of the court must have been another Conkling man. "Gentlemen of the jury," he intoned as if the whole proceeding was perfectly normal, "hearken to the verdict as the court hath recorded it. You say you find the defendant guilty of the offense charged. So say you all."

The twelve jurymen looked stunned. They had not even met to discuss the case, much less agree on a verdict. When Henry Selden asked if the clerk could at least poll the jury, Judge Hunt rapped his gavel sharply and declared, "That cannot be allowed. Gentlemen of the jury, you are discharged."

An enraged Henry Selden lost no time in introducing a motion for a new trial on the grounds that his client had been denied the right to a jury verdict. Judge Hunt denied the motion. He turned to Susan B. Anthony and said, "The prisoner will stand up. Has the prisoner anything to say why sentence shall not be pronounced?"

Thus far in the trial, Susan B. Anthony had remained silent. Now, she rose to her feet and said slowly, "Yes, your honor, I have many things to say."

Without further preliminaries, she launched into a scathing denunciation of Judge Hunt's conduct of her trial. ". . . In your ordered verdict of guilty," she said, "you have trampled underfoot every vital principle of our government. My natural rights, my civil rights, my political rights, are all alike ignored. Robbed of the fundamental privilege of citizenship, I am degraded from the status of a citizen to that of a subject; and not only myself individually, but all of my sex, are, by your honor's verdict, doomed to political subjection under this so-called Republican government."

Judge Hunt reached for his gavel, but Susan B. Anthony refused to be silenced.

"May it please your honor," she continued. "Your denial of my citizen's right to vote is the denial of my right to a trial by a jury of my peers as an offender against law, therefore, the denial of my sacred rights to life, liberty, property, and—"

"The court cannot allow the prisoner to go on," Judge Hunt cried out.

Susan ignored him and continued her impassioned tirade against the court. Hunt frantically rapped his gavel and ordered her to sit down and be quiet. But Susan, who must have been taking delight in his consternation, kept on talking. She deplored the fact that she had been denied the right to a fair trial. Even if she had been given such a trial, she insisted, it would not have been by her peers. Jury, judges, and lawyers were not her equals, but her superiors, because they could vote and she could not. Susan was adamant about the fact that she had been denied the justice guaranteed in the Constitution to every citizen of the United States.

Judge Hunt was sufficiently cowed by now to try to defend himself. "The prisoner has been tried according to the established forms of law," he sputtered.

"Yes, your honor," retorted Susan, overlooking his blatant lie, "but by forms of law all made by men, interpreted by men, administered by men, in favor of men, and against women; and hence your honor's ordered verdict of guilty, against a United States citizen for the exercise of that citizen's right to vote, simply because that citizen was a woman and not a man. But yesterday, the same manmade forms of law declared it a crime punishable with a one-thousand-dollar fine and six months imprisonment, for you, or me, or any of us, to give a cup of cold water, a crust of bread, or a night's shelter to a panting fugitive while he was tracking his way to Canada. And every man or woman in whose veins coursed a drop of human sympathy violated that wicked law, reckless of consequences, and was justified in so doing. As, then, the slaves who got their freedom must take it over, or under, or through the unjust forms of law, precisely so now must women, to get their right to a voice in this government, take it, and I have taken mine, and mean to take it at every opportunity."

Judge Hunt flailed his gavel and gave the by now futile order for the prisoner to sit down and be quiet. Susan kept right on talking.

"When I was brought before your honor for trial," she said, "I hoped for a broad and liberal interpretation of the Constitution and its recent Amendments. One that would declare all United States citizens under its protection. But failing to get this justice—failing, even, to get a trial by a jury *not* of my peers—I ask not leniency at your hands—but to take the full rigors of the law."

With that Susan finally obeyed Judge Hunt's orders and sat down. Now he had to reverse himself and order her to stand up so he could impose sentence. As soon as he pronounced the sentence—a fine of one hundred dollars plus the costs of prosecuting the trial—Susan spoke up again. "May it please your honor," she said, "I shall never pay a dollar of your unjust penalty. All the stock in trade I possess is a ten-thousand-dollar debt, incurred by publishing my paper—*The Revolution*—four years ago, the sole object of which was to educate all women to do precisely as I have done, rebel against your manmade, unjust, unconstitutional forms of law, that tax, fine, imprison, and hang women, while they deny them the right of representation in the government; and I shall work on with might and main to pay every dollar of that honest debt, but not a penny shall go to this unjust claim. And I shall earnestly and persistently continue to urge all women to the practical recognition of the old Revolutionary maxim, that 'Resistance to tyranny is obedience to God.' "

Judge Hunt must have had strict orders not only to see that the defendant was convicted, but to do everything he could to prevent the case from going on to a higher court. He allowed Susan to walk out of the courtroom without imposing a prison sentence in lieu of her unpaid fine. If he had sent her to prison, she could have been released on a writ of habeas corpus and would have had the right to appeal. As it was, the case was closed.

Although she was disappointed that her case would not go to the Supreme Court as she had originally hoped, Susan knew that she had struck an important blow for woman's suffrage. Henry Selden's arguments and her own speech at the end of the trial were widely publicized, and Judge Hunt's conduct of the trial stood as proof that women were treated unjustly before the law.

Susan did not forget the election inspectors who had allowed her to cast her ballot. The men were fined twenty-five dollars each and sent to jail when they refused to pay. In all, they spent about a week behind bars before Susan, through the influence of friends in Washington, obtained presidential pardons for each of them. In the meantime, her followers, who included some of the best cooks in Rochester, saw to it that the men were supplied with delicious hot meals and home-baked pies.

True to her promise, Susan paid the legal expenses for the three inspectors. With the help of contributions from sympathetic admirers, she paid the costs of her own trial. But she never paid that one-hundred-dollar fine. Susan B. Anthony was a woman of her word as well as a woman of courage.

The Voice of a Race

If I had my way, Susan B. Anthony would have fought her case all the way to the Supreme Court and won, and Elizabeth Blackwell would have made some marvelous medical discovery that would have had the whole world singing the praises of women doctors.

As you can see, I like happy—perhaps a better word is *triumphant*—endings. That's why I've always taken great satisfaction in the way one American woman, Marian Anderson, succeeded in scoring a dramatic victory against her enemies.

Marian Anderson wins my vote as a woman of fortitude for several reasons. Not the least of these is the way she set her sights on becoming a concert singer. It's a difficult goal at best, but for Marian Anderson, it was doubly difficult because of the color of her skin. She found this out soon after she graduated from high school.

Marian had been studying music privately for several years, and her teacher felt that she was ready for the kind of training that could be had only at a conservatory. Luckily, there was an outstanding conservatory not far from her home in Philadelphia. Marian decided to enroll.

She arrived at the music school on registration day and, after patiently waiting in the long line of other applicants, reached the desk where a young woman was handing out registration forms. The woman looked past Marian and motioned to the young man behind her to step forward. Not until everyone in the line had received an application did she finally turn to Marian Anderson.

"What do you want?" she snapped.

Marian said that she wanted an application. The young woman replied curtly, "We don't take colored."

It seems incredible that the woman who turned out to be one of the most magnificent singers of the twentieth century was denied an opportunity to study voice because of her race, but discrimination was a way of life in this country for more years than most of us like to admit.

Marian Anderson's career as a musician might have ended that day if it were not for the gift of strength she received from a woman who knew nothing about music. Her mother, Annie Anderson, did not look or act the part of a strong woman. Small and quiet, she never raised her voice. She had lost her husband when Marian was still in grade school and had supported her three daughters by working as a cleaning woman in Wanamaker's, Philadelphia's leading department store. More than once, she almost collapsed from exhaustion—but Marian never heard a word of complaint from her mother's lips. Annie Anderson was a woman of faith, and she offered that patient faith to her troubled daughter.

Calmly, she told Marian that "someone would be raised up" to help her accomplish what she had hoped to do at the conservatory. A few weeks later, a fellow singer introduced her to Giuseppe Boghetti, one of Philadelphia's outstanding voice teachers. He heard her sing "Deep River" and said: "I will make room for you right away."

CULVER PICTURES INC.

Marian Anderson in her moment of triumph in front of the Lincoln Memorial on Easter Sunday morning, 1939. Over 75,000 people came to hear this historic performance.

But Marian Anderson still needed large reserves of her mother's faith to cope with another aspect of a black singer's life. Whenever she traveled south to give a concert, she was forced to ride in the Jim Crow car of the train. Inevitably, it was filthy and badly lit, and even if she did succeed in prying open one of its grimy windows, it was only to be met with a blast of soot from the engine just ahead.

The aspiring artist was treated to an even worse sample of segregation one day when she asked the porter if she and her accompanist could get a hot meal in the dining car. The porter, who was black himself, arranged for a table, but Marian and her pianist had to sit at the end of the dining car and eat behind drawn curtains as if they were lepers or two-headed freaks.

Marian Anderson often worried about the effects of discrimination on her fellow blacks. She had studied the faces around her in the Jim Crow car. Some were embarrassed, some were resigned, some were too defeated to care. The young singer could see that there was a desperate need for change in America's attitude toward her black citizens, but she never saw herself as the torchbearer of that change. She had elected to give her life to music; someone else would have to take up the cudgels against racial injustice.

Marian Anderson also preferred her mother's way of patient trust in God. "Mother's religion made her believe that she would receive what is right for her to have if she was conscientious in her faith," Marian says. "If it did not come, it was because He had not considered it right for her. We grew in this atmosphere of faith that she created, aware that Mother had a strength beyond the energies of her small body. We believed as she did because we wanted the same kind of haven in the time of storm."

Marian Anderson needed this faith for still another

reason. Getting to the top of the musical world was an agonizingly slow process. I've often thought that anyone who opts for a career in the performing arts (myself included) must be some sort of masochist. It takes a tremendous amount of hard work and training before you can even hope to reach the top. Even then, some of the best trained and most disciplined performers never achieve stardom.

Marian Anderson spent more than ten years in the musical minor leagues. At one point in 1925, she thought she had made a breakthrough. She entered a contest for unknown singers and was chosen from among three hundred competitors to appear in Lewisohn Stadium with the New York Philharmonic Orchestra. The reviewers were kind, but after this one brush with success, her career was again becalmed. She went back to performing in third-rate auditoriums and struggling through a dreary round of invitations from glee clubs, choirs, and fraternal organizations.

Like many American performers, Marian Anderson had to go to Europe to be discovered. A Berlin concert manager, no more enthusiastic about her talents than her own countrymen had been, signed her up for a tour of the European concert stage. To his amazement, she was a sensation. Before long, she was giving command performances before the kings of Sweden and Denmark. The Finnish composer Jean Sibelius wrote the song "Solitude" in her honor, and the maestro Arturo Toscanini, who attended one of her concerts in Salzburg, declared that a voice like hers came along only once in a hundred years.

When Marian Anderson returned to her native country in 1935, it was under the management of the world-famous impresario Sol Hurok. She had, at last, reached the top.

Marian Anderson's concert tour of the United States

began with two appearances at Carnegie Hall. Both were sellouts. Yet even as her career curved upward, race prejudice still inflicted small, mean wounds. When she appeared at Carnegie Hall, for instance, not a single hotel in midtown Manhattan would rent her a room. In another city, the local concert manager did not meet her at the train or call on her at her hotel. He did not see her, in fact, until he appeared backstage minutes before curtain time and pointedly declined to shake hands. Marian said nothing. She just went out and sang. That was her rule. Not to fight but to perform.

Some years later, Sol Hurok gleefully told the denouement of this little tale: "The second time Marian arrived in that city, the local manager met her at the station in his own car. He shook hands with her when she stepped off the train, escorted her himself to her hotel. He fetched her to the auditorium for her rehearsal and drove her up and down the streets of his city that afternoon, showing her the local sights. He drove her to the concert in the evening, and the next morning he drove her in his own car to the next stop on her itinerary, which happened to be in a neighboring town."

Marian Anderson's stupendous talent had prompted more than a few racists to overcome their prejudice. As her career soared, invitations for concerts began to pour in. Sol Hurok was determined to have her appear in the best concert hall of every leading city in the country. He was understandably delighted when Howard University asked to sponsor a Marian Anderson concert in Washington, D. C. Hurok agreed, and in January, 1939, the manager of Howard University's concert series filed an application to reserve the capital's foremost platform, Constitution Hall. This seemingly routine request catapulted the singer into a tremendous racial and political uproar. Before it was over, Marian Anderson would win an imperishable place in the tradition of American women of courage.

The manager of Constitution Hall informed the Howard University representative that the auditorium was not available. A clause in the rental contract prohibited the presentation of Negro artists. The clause had been put there by the Daughters of the American Revolution, who owned the hall, tax-free.

Marian Anderson reacted to the D. A. R.'s rebuff with characteristic fortitude. Her mother, a woman of unswerving faith, had often told her "that right will win . . . that a way will be found." Her words had given Marian the strength to go on studying even after her rejection by the Philadelphia conservatory. This same faith had sustained her every time she was insulted or ignored because of her race.

Although Marian Anderson was saddened to learn that she was being barred from Constitution Hall, she refused to brood about the incident. She was on tour and she owed it to her audiences to think about nothing but her music. Negotiations for halls were Mr. Hurok's business.

In Washington, the treasurer of Howard University wrote an open letter to the newspapers protesting the D. A. R.'s unconscionable policy. As far as Howard University and Marian Anderson were concerned, that would have been the end of the matter. In 1939, Jim Crow still ruled Washington, D. C., and the rest of America's South. Much as they hated it, few blacks saw any hope of changing the status quo. But a long list of white Americans who knew and admired Marian Anderson were eager to spring to her defense.

At the head of this list was Sol Hurok. He inserted himself into the dispute with a letter to the manager of Constitution Hall, asking him to waive the restrictive clause for Marian Anderson "so as not to deny to the people of Washington a great musical experience."

The manager replied that Constitution Hall was not available on the date requested by Howard University, April 9, and advised Mr. Hurok to communicate directly with the Daughters of the American Revolution. When Hurok did so, he was politely told that the hall was "already engaged." Hurok next asked if the eighth or tenth of April was open. The answer came back: "The Hall is not available for a concert by Miss Anderson."

Crackles of indignation began to be heard in the musical world. Lawrence Tibbett, one of the stars of the Metropolitan Opera, and at that time president of the American Guild of Musical Artists, wired the president-general of the D. A. R. asking how "the daughters of those who fought for the establishment of this great democracy" could perpetuate "such an obviously undemocratic and un-American rule."

The violinist Jascha Heifetz appeared in the Hall but told reporters afterward that he felt "uncomfortable" on the platform. It pained him to think that he was playing where "a great singer has been barred because of her race." But these protests went relatively unheard until a more powerful voice spoke out.

It was February 28, 1939. Marian Anderson was in San Francisco for a concert. As usual, she spent the day in seclusion, but as she left her hotel that evening, she happened to glance at a newsstand. A headline caught her eye: "MRS. ROOSEVELT TAKES STAND." Below, in smaller type was a report that Eleanor Roosevelt had resigned from the Daughters of the American Revolution. Marian Anderson did not have to read any further to know why. But, true to her singer's creed, she did not buy a copy of the paper. She wanted nothing on her mind now, only an hour before curtain time, but her music.

At the concert hall she gave her usual superb performance to the usual enthusiastic full house. Only upon returning to the hotel did she buy a newspaper. It told her exactly what she had suspected and dreaded. Her private war with the D. A. R. had escalated into a full-scale conflict in which everyone in the country would be forced to take sides.

Eleanor Roosevelt's action, and Marian Anderson's reaction, present a study in two equally admirable, but nevertheless very different types of courage. If Mrs. Roosevelt had been a general, she would have favored the bold frontal assault. Marian Anderson, on the other hand, would have been the kind of military leader who concentrates on building up superior strength and then lies back and lets the enemy try in vain to defeat her.

From the beginning of her career as First Lady, Mrs. Roosevelt had consistently spoken out on behalf of black Americans in spite of fierce opposition from powerful men close to her husband who were afraid that she would damage the President politically. Only a few weeks before the uproar over Constitution Hall began, Mrs. Roosevelt had attended the Southern Conference on Human Welfare, which met in Birmingham, Alabama. The city fathers had decreed that white and black delegates must sit in separate parts of the hall. Mrs. Roosevelt insisted that her chair be placed in the aisle between the two groups. This may not seem like a particularly daring gesture now, but in a southern city in the 1930s, it took nerve. The National Conference of Negro Youths passed a resolution thanking Eleanor Roosevelt for her moral courage.

Mrs. Roosevelt's decision to take a stand in the Constitution Hall controversy stemmed from this same commitment to civil rights, but this time she had an even more personal stake in the struggle. For one thing, she was a member of the Daughters of the American Revolution. For another, she knew Marian Anderson. In February, 1936, shortly after the singer returned from Europe, the First Lady had invited her to sing at the White House.

More than once in the past, Mrs. Roosevelt had debated whether to publicly resign from an organization that offended her sense of justice. She had quit the exclusive Colony Club in New York when they blackballed Elinor Morgenthau, wife of the Secretary of the Treasury, because she was Jewish. But she had done so quietly. This time, she decided to announce her resignation, and the reasons for it, in public.

"In the past when I was able to work actively in any organization to which I belonged," she explained in her syndicated news column "My Day," "I've usually stayed in until I had at least made a fight and been defeated. Even then I have as a rule accepted my defeat and decided either that I was wrong or that I was perhaps a little too far ahead of the thinking of the majority at that time. . . . But in this case I belong to an organization in which I can do no active work. They have taken an action which has been widely talked about in the press. To remain as a member implies approval of that action, and therefore I am resigning."

Within twenty-four hours, everyone in the country was talking about the episode. At that point in her long career in public life, many of Eleanor Roosevelt's liberal attitudes were applauded only by a small band of stalwarts. Her resignation from the D. A. R. met with the approval of moderates and conservatives as well.

"I want you to know how proud I was of you the other day," wrote one of Mrs. Roosevelt's staunchly Republican, violently anti-New Deal cousins. Dr. Endicott Peabody, headmaster of her husband's alma mater, the exclusive Groton School, told her, "Your courage in taking this definite stand called for my admiration."

To Marian Anderson, who had always avoided making an issue of her race, the experience was nightmarish. She was still on tour, and in every city she visited, newspapermen mobbed her, trying to get a comment. She refused to say a word. In the past, this kind of fortitude had stood her in good stead. She had been able to ignore her detractors and take refuge in her music until the pain subsided. But the uproar over Constitution Hall refused to die down. In fact, it seemed to increase and to follow Marian Anderson wherever she went.

Expressions of sympathy and support poured in from all sides, but Marian Anderson still refused to get angry or feel sorry for herself. If it had been up to her, she would have tried to find a way to wipe out the bitterness that the incident was causing. This did not mean that she felt she was not entitled to appear in Constitution Hall. She thoroughly disapproved of the D. A. R.'s restrictive clause. But it would have been totally out of character for her to strike out against her enemies.

"I had been in this world long enough to know that there are all kinds of people, all suited by their own natures for different tasks," she says. "It would be fooling myself to think that I was meant to be a fearless fighter; I was not, just as I was not meant to be a soprano instead of a contralto."

For a while, it looked as if Marian Anderson would not have to be a fighter. Her supporters, who had by now grown into a formidable army, were doing the fighting for her.

Howard University had asked the Washington, D. C.,

Board of Education if the concert could be held in the Central High School auditorium. Washington's schools were segregated, and at first the board refused. But the Marian Anderson Protest Committee stepped forward with a petition signed by thousands of individuals and organizations from all over the country. The board relented, but not completely. Marian Anderson could sing in Central High School—but only before an all-white audience.

An infuriated Sol Hurok stepped into the picture once more. Ever the showman, Hurok announced that Marian Anderson would appear in Washington, D. C., without the help of the Daughters of the American Revolution or the Board of Education. She would sing outdoors and admission would be free to people of every race, creed, and color.

Hurok sent his press agent to Washington to settle the details. Walter White, national secretary of the NAACP, who had been working closely with Mrs. Roosevelt since the struggle began, steered him to Assistant Secretary of the Interior Oscar L. Chapman. Oscar is one of my favorite people. He handled the advance planning for my father's campaign in 1948. A more intelligent and delightful man I have never met.

Oscar Chapman was completely in favor of Sol Hurok's idea of an outdoor concert. But it was not an easy matter to decide just where in Washington such a concert could be held. Walter White suggested Lafayette Park, opposite the White House. Oscar shook his head. The park was too small. Besides, they would have to station troops around the White House to guarantee presidential security.

For a moment everyone was stymied. Then Oscar got the brainstorm of the year. "What if we used the Lincoln Memorial on Easter Sunday?" When Walter White expressed his enthusiasm for the idea, Oscar called in Felix Cohen, one of the brightest lawyers in Washington, to ask if there were any legal obstacles to the plan. "I would gamble my reputation that there is nothing that stands in your way except courage," said Cohen.

From then on, it was full speed ahead. Oscar went to Secretary of the Interior Harold Ickes, who instantly approved the idea, and rushed to the White House to catch FDR as he was leaving for Warm Springs. The President gave his approval and Oscar, Walter White, and Eleanor Roosevelt immediately began organizing a sponsoring committee. They agreed that it would be better if Mrs. Roosevelt moved to the sidelines to reduce the intensity of the controversy. To replace her, she suggested an old friend, New York's Congresswoman-at-large, Caroline O'Day.

While the politicians organized, Marian Anderson tried to keep singing. She still had a number of important concerts on her schedule, but wherever she went, she was greeted by reporters hoping to persuade her to say hostile things about the D. A. R. She consistently refused. Her fortitude was impressive, but as the plans for the concert at the Lincoln Memorial escalated, she began to be aware of a frightening reality. Felix Cohen had told Oscar Chapman: "There is nothing that stands in your way except courage." But the largest portion of that courage would have to be supplied by a lonely woman who had devoted her life to the creation of great music, not to the hand-to-hand combat the reporters and politicians were urging on her.

Marian Anderson discussed her fears about the situation with the one woman she had been close to all her life. Annie Anderson told her that no one could make the decision but herself.

"Mother knew what that decision would be," Marian Anderson says. "In my heart I also knew. I could not run away from the situation. I had become, whether I liked it or not, a symbol, representing my people. I had to appear."

Her time of storm had come, and the faith that her mother had given her, not by preaching but by a lifetime of example, sustained her. As Marian put it so beautifully in her autobiography, *My Lord, What a Morning,* "I had to decide where I would find the new strength I needed. I found it where Mother had always found hers."

But the decision did not mean that she was henceforth immune to fears and doubts. Like other women (and men) of courage as they faced their crises, Marian Anderson wavered. At midnight on Easter Saturday, she telephoned Sol Hurok and asked, "Must we really go through with this?" Marian knew the answer even before she asked the question. The mere fact that she asked it, has never denied asking it, is one more proof of her right to be called a woman of courage.

Marian Anderson arrived in Washington the next morning. A police guard with shrieking sirens escorted her through the quiet Sunday streets to the home of Gifford Pinchot, the former Governor of Pennsylvania. The Pinchots had offered their house when they learned that no Washington hotel would accept the singer and her party. Like a true professional, Marian next drove to the Lincoln Memorial with her accompanist, Kosti Vehanen. He tried out the piano, and they examined the public address system with its battery of six microphones. Then she returned to the Pinchots' and spent the next few hours studying her music while an immense crowd gathered around the Lincoln Memorial.

When Marian Anderson returned that afternoon, there were seventy-five thousand people—about half of them black, half white—before the Memorial and around both sides of the reflecting pool. The crowd stretched almost down to the Washington Monument at its opposite end. The sight of this enormous murmuring assembly was a shock. "I had sensations unlike any I had experienced before," Marian recalls. "My heart beat wildly, and I could not talk. I even wondered whether I would be able to sing."

Police opened a passage through the crowd, and the singer was led to a small room inside the monument where Secretary of the Interior Harold Ickes was waiting to greet her. Outside on the platform were some of the most prestigious men in Washington—Cabinet members, a Supreme Court Justice, an assortment of senators and representatives.

But these politicians, and even the committee who had done so much to make this concert possible, were no longer important. It was Marian Anderson's hour. Her eyes flashed for one brief compelling moment at the great marble figure of Abraham Lincoln, the lines of sorrow etched in his huge face. Then, composed and ready, she stepped out on the platform and looked out at that sea of people.

It had taken enormous strength for Marian Anderson to muster the courage for this unique performance. Now, before she had even sung a note, she felt that courage renewed and quickened by the unspoken enthusiasm of her audience. "I had a feeling that a great wave of goodwill poured out from these people, almost engulfing me," she says. "When I stood up to sing our national anthem I felt for a moment as though I were choking. For a desperate second I thought that the words, well as I knew them, would not come."

But they came. How they came! From the national anthem Marian went on to sing six of her favorite songs. First was "America." Then, "O mio Fernando" from the Donizetti opera, *La Favorita,* the song she had sung in her first important appearance—at Lewisohn Stadium in New

York fourteen long years ago. Then came the song that is one of her personal favorites, Schubert's "Ave Maria." Finally, there were three spirituals, "Gospel Train," "Trampin'," and "My Soul Is Anchored in the Lord." As the moving words and the marvelous melody of these songs poured from Marian Anderson's throat, she became, in the words of one critic, "the voice of a race."

The words of "Trampin'" were especially poignant for black Americans in 1939.

> I'm trampin', I'm trampin',
> I'm trying to make Heaven my home.
> I've never been to Heaven but I've been told
> That the streets up there are paved with gold.

As she sang these words, Marian Anderson saw "an army of people who were bowed down and whose only solace was the march along the road to Heaven—to the things they never had."

To Sol Hurok, a man who had sat through a thousand concerts, it was the most memorable moment of his life. "We were not merely sung to, we were exalted," he said. He could see that exaltation shining on the faces of seventy-five thousand Americans in the audience.

As the last lines of "My Soul Is Anchored in the Lord" died away, the crowd erupted. It was not applause, it was tumult, a wild mixture of cheering and pounding hands and stamping feet. Marian Anderson was so overcome by emotion that she had to look in the newspapers the next day to discover what she had said in response. Her speech had been brief. "I am overwhelmed," she had said. "I just can't talk. I can't tell you what you have done for me today. I thank you from the bottom of my heart again and again."

It was the truth, but behind those words lay another truth. A woman of fortitude had forced the American people to confront the greatest, most shameful inequity in our national life. Marian Anderson had made her voice the symbol of the too long forgotten doctrine that all men are created equal.

Part IV

Gallant Voices

To most people, the word *gallantry* conjures up visions of knights on white chargers riding off to some holy war, or noblemen fighting duels to defend the honor of their king and country. But I happen to think that gallantry, without its storybook trappings, is still very much alive in our present day.

Gallantry is essentially courage in the pursuit of high ideals. In our lexicon, however, courage is too often equated with risking one's life, and high ideals encompass only the loftiest goals. People rarely see anything gallant in doing one's job or listening to one's conscience, but oddly enough, that is where gallantry is most apt to be needed.

As more than a few Americans have discovered, there are times when a person may be under pressure *not* to do his job, times when he may be asked, and expected, to go along with practices that violate his personal code of conduct.

I say "his" because the problem is encountered more often by men than by women. But the few women who have managed to achieve positions of responsibility in business or government have, on occasion, found themselves confronting the same hard choices: whether to acquiesce to something they know is wrong or to risk their jobs, and possibly their reputations, by saying no. I'm happy to say that a significant number of women preferred to say no.

I have often puzzled over the reasons for their courage. Women, particularly in the past, have had to work so much harder than men to achieve the same positions, one might expect them to be far more loath to jeopardize them. On the other hand, I suppose that the women who fought their way into the upper echelons were used to going against the crowd. How else could they have achieved their goals?

I can't help feeling, however, that the courage displayed by American women in adhering to their ideals has, to a large extent, been prompted by a strongly, although not exclusively, feminine quality—caring. It is as if these women brought to their careers the same fierce sense of concern they might exhibit on the smaller, more intimate, level of family living. Few of them set out to be crusaders, but almost all of them felt an obligation, when the situation warranted, to serve as voices of humanity in the sometimes inhuman welter of accepted codes and customs.

The women who chose to give caring a prominent place in their careers knew even before they began that their voices might go unheard. They were aware that idealism is often rewarded with frustration and failure. But I doubt that any of them foresaw the difficulties they would encounter in fulfilling those two apparently simple obligations —doing their jobs and following their consciences. When you hear what those difficulties were and see how courageously they endured them, I think you'll agree with me that gallantry has by no means gone out of style.

The Good Angel of Oklahoma

For a few brief years at the beginning of this century, Kate Barnard was a power to be reckoned with in Oklahoma politics.

A small, pretty woman with olive skin, black hair, and deep blue eyes, Kate appeared on the political scene in 1907 just as the "twin territories"—Oklahoma and several former Indian reservations—were about to merge and become our forty-sixth state. It was a rare opportunity to mold the future, and Kate Barnard played a major role in the drama. A new commonwealth was about to be formed, a new constitution written. Kate Barnard was determined that this constitution would aid Oklahoma's poor and dispossessed—especially their children.

An intense sympathy for the losers, the dropouts, the failures of our competitive society burned deep in Kate Barnard's spirit. One reason was her own unhappy childhood. Her mother died when she was only eighteen months old, and her father, a surveyor, left her with relatives on a lonely Kansas farm while he traveled throughout the West on assignments. When John Barnard purchased 160 acres of land in what was still the territory of Oklahoma, he brought his sixteen-year-old daughter to homestead it with him—but left her on the farm with a few hired hands for months at a time while he continued his surveying career. This meant more loneliness. There was an element of desperation in the fervent love Kate often professed for her footloose father. In her long days alone, she sometimes dreamt of doing something bold and heroic which would win his admiration. It is easy to see why she was instinctively sympathetic to anyone—especially children—who lacked a caring parent or friend. She knew only too well the hollow ache of that pain.

Kate thought happiness had finally arrived when she and her father moved to Oklahoma City in 1892. But Mr. Barnard chose to settle on land he owned in one of the city's slums—where Kate got her first glimpse of mass misery. Not everyone who followed the frontier was a self-reliant Daniel Boone-Davy Crockett type. A dismaying number were failures who thought geography was the answer to their woes. But they only repeated their dismal performance in a new locale, and their wives and children remained victims of poverty's grinding humiliation and deprivation.

Kate wrote a series of letters to the *Daily Oklahoman*, describing the grim life of the city's poor and asking the blunt question: what was Oklahoma City going to do about it? The well-to-do responded by practically burying Kate in no fewer than ten thousand garments and a mountain of furniture. She and a small group of women associates found four hundred destitute children, many of them living in tents, gave them the clothing, bought books for them, and sent them to school. Church and business leaders meanwhile were forming a Provident Association. They offered Kate the job of matron. She accepted—but immediately demonstrated that she was not satisfied to be a lady bountiful.

While she continued to give away food and clothing, Kate organized Oklahoma City's unemployed into a labor union. She found jobs for four hundred of her members

I see fragility as well as courage in this sensitive portrait of Kate Barnard when she was at the height of her power and influence in Oklahoma.

and became their delegate to the State Federation of Labor. From there it was only a step to her election as a delegate to the "Shawnee Convention"—an uneasy coalition of farm and labor representatives who met to form a united front in the upcoming election, which would decide who wrote the new state's constitution.

Kate's emergence as a political power began when she persuaded the workers and farmers to adopt resolutions calling for compulsory education and the abolition of child labor, and demanding the creation of a Department of Charities and Corrections to supervise the state's social welfare programs. All three proposals became major planks in the Democratic party platform, and Kate hurled herself into the campaign to elect Democratic delegates to the constitutional convention. Her strong voice and dramatic, earnest delivery made her an excellent public speaker. Thanks largely to her eloquence, Oklahoma, once considered a Republican stronghold, elected no fewer than ninety-eight Democrats—and only nine Republicans—to the constitutional convention.

The convention met in the fall of 1906, and the Democrats, needless to say, had the upper hand. The compulsory education and child labor provisions won almost unanimous approval, and Kate's other pet project, the creation of a state Department of Charities and Corrections, was also adopted. The official description of the department's Commissioner referred to "his" or "her" office. Thus it came as no great surprise when the Democrats nominated Kate for the job. For a while the Republicans considered endorsing her too, but they finally settled for another woman candidate, who must have known from the beginning that she was destined to lose.

Kate's popularity combined with her gifts as a public speaker made her virtually unbeatable. She attracted record turnouts wherever she spoke, and dozens of lesser candidates begged her to appear on their programs to ensure a crowd.

Kate looked sweet and demure, but there was an inner toughness beneath her charm. On one occasion, she was scheduled to speak in a town where fifteen coal miners had recently been burned to death because of inadequate safety conditions at the mine. The town fathers warned her not to come, but Kate went anyway. When she arrived, all the public halls suddenly became unavailable. Unintimidated, Kate staged her rally on a street corner.

As soon as she began to speak, the negligent mine owner pushed his way to the front of the crowd and stood there, arms folded, glaring at her. He was a thick-necked barrel of a man with a violent temper. He had obviously used this tactic in the past to silence other visiting speakers. But it did not work with Kate Barnard. She glared right back at him, and tossed aside her prepared speech.

Pointing her finger at the mine owner, she said:

> The diamonds you are wearing in your shirt front were bought with the blood of fifteen men who were burned to death in a mine which you own, because you would not spend the money to provide two entrances. You made their wives widows; you made their children orphans; you are responsible to Almighty God for the long, weary lives of poverty and ignorance which they face; and if the people of this state of Oklahoma will elect me to the office which I am seeking I will change such conditions, not only in your mine, but in all others.

There were more miners in Oklahoma than mine owners, more Democrats than Republicans, and, as it turned out, more Kate Barnard fans than even her staunchest supporters had suspected. In Oklahoma's first election as a new state in 1907, Kate made political history. She polled six thousand more votes than any other Democrat on the ticket and at the age of thirty-two became the first woman in the United States to be elected to a statewide office.

The new Commissioner of Charities and Corrections tried to make Oklahoma the most progressive state in the union. She knew the experts in every field that came under her jurisdiction—reform schools, insane asylums, training programs for the handicapped, medical care for the poor. Each expert was invited to Oklahoma and given a chance to present his ideas to the state legislature. Then Kate went to work, pushing and prodding the lawmakers until the ideas were voted into realities.

Kate Barnard soon ranked among the experts herself. She traveled around the country addressing social workers' and teachers' associations, political and labor groups. Again and again she stressed the importance of better care for widows, orphans, the unemployed.

The early years of the twentieth century—the Progressive Era—were a period of tremendous social awareness. There were demands for reform in practically every area of American life, from government and industry to the design and furnishing of homes. Kate was in favor of most of the reforms, with one surprising exception. She had no interest in woman's suffrage. "The boys always do what I ask them," she said, "so I don't see any need to go to the polls myself." Kate may have been saying that she saw no reason to insert a highly explosive issue into her Oklahoma bailiwick when things were going well. Like a good politician, she was willing to compromise on some issues, to win on more important ones. But Oklahoma would soon discover that there were some issues on which Kate Barnard would never compromise.

For years, Kate Barnard's support was the decisive factor in Oklahoma City's mayoralty elections. She would campaign for whichever candidate, Democrat or Republican, was likely to do the most for the poor. But campaigning was only one of her assets. On Election Day, she would make a personal tour of the slums. Whenever she saw a saloonkeeper herding a group of barflies off to the polls, Kate would sail up to them with a cheerful smile. "Hello, boys," she'd say innocently. "Where are you going?"

While the saloonkeeper, who was being paid to muster the votes for the opposition, stood there growling helplessly, Kate would give the would-be voters a brief speech on behalf of her man. Along the way, she would mention the jobs she had found for Pete and Mike, remind Joe that she had helped get the doctor when his wife was so sick, and ask if Gus's daughter was doing better in school now that she had new eyeglasses.

Kate was no less adept at manipulating state legislators. Not long after she took office, a group of her original supporters decided that the six-thousand-dollar appropriation for the Department of Charities and Corrections was far too large. The Speaker of the House, a double-crossing Democrat, I regret to report, became the leader of the move to slash it. He announced that he would vote only for Kate's salary and the salary of a stenographer.

Kate went to work and within a week had seventy-eight legislators behind her. By the time the budget cut was introduced, the Speaker was being bombarded with every imaginable accusation from dishonesty to simple-mindedness. A prominent Democrat gave a stirring speech in which he extolled Kate Barnard's accomplishments and hailed her as "the good angel of Oklahoma." The leader of the Republican minority declared himself ready to give her ten thousand dollars more than the original appropriation if she would only say the word. The debate ended with one thousand dollars being added to Kate's budget and the Speaker utterly humiliated. The appropriation passed with only five dissenting votes.

The work of the Commissioner of Charities and Corrections covered every aspect of social welfare. Kate rounded up homeless children and saw that they were housed and fed and sent to school; she battled for safety laws in mines and factories and explored new ways of educating the deaf, the dumb, and the blind. One of her major interests was prison reform. In the summer of 1909, she barged into the Kansas State Prison, where Oklahoma convicts were being kept under a contract system, and demanded to be taken on an inspection tour. She discovered that the prisoners were being grossly overworked and horrendously mistreated. The guards had devised a number of inhuman punishments. One was binding and gagging a man, smearing his face with molasses, and then leaving him beside an open window where flies and other insects could get at him. Another was tying a man's hands and feet behind his back until they met, then sealing him face down in a heavy coffin.

Kate issued a devastating report of her findings. In the wake of the scandal it caused, Oklahoma was inspired to build its own model penitentiary and Kansas convicts won some badly needed prison reforms.

Kate Barnard was reelected by a large majority in 1910. But her second term had barely begun when she found herself confronted by a test of her courage and her conscience that forced her to fight some of the most powerful men in both her own Democratic party and in the Republican party. The trouble started when a report came into the Department of Charities that three "elf" children were living in a field just outside of town. They slept in the hollow of an old tree and got their food by begging at nearby farmhouses. Kate sent one of her assistants to find the trio and bring them back to her office.

The three elves turned out to be Indian children. They were a sorry sight. Their clothes were filthy rags, their arms and legs were scrawny and covered with scabs, their black hair was so tangled and matted that it resisted comb and brush and had to be cut away from their scalps.

The youngsters were sent to a children's shelter while Kate set about finding out who they were. After six weeks of investigation, she turned up the fact that their parents had died a few years before and they had been placed under the protection of a guardian. The man had also been appointed guardian for some fifty-one other Indian minors. When Kate asked him where the other children were, he shrugged indifferently. "I don't know," he murmured. "I've lost all track of them."

What made the situation even more appalling was another discovery by Kate's investigators. The three Indian children owned valuable lands in the Glenn Pool oilfields. The guardian had been collecting their rents and keeping them for himself. Kate did not even try to conceal her contempt. The man who stood before her was worse than a common thief.

Kate was horrified to discover that defrauding Indians had become a popular and profitable pastime in Oklahoma. It was the denouement of a national policy that was launched in 1887 as a brilliant answer to the "Indian problem." Reformers had persuaded a reluctant Congress to pass it. Under the so-called "severalty" plan, the tribal lands were divided up, and plots of up to 160 acres parceled out to individual Indians. The goal was the abolition of the reservation, which the reformers of that era saw as a "city of destruction." Owning private property, these simple-minded do-gooders thought, would automatically turn Indians into white men. This was supposed to be progress back in the days when white supremacy was taken for granted by almost every Caucasian American. No one stopped to realize that private property was an idea almost wholly foreign to Indian thinking. Nor did anyone worry about the social consequences of destroying the tribal communities that gave most Indians their sense of identity.

Originally, the federal government was supposed to hold the land in trust for each Indian for twenty-five years. But in response to cries about "getting the government out of the Indian business," federal officials transferred the responsibility for Indian minors to Oklahoma's probate courts. Many of these children were immensely wealthy. Coal had been discovered on the Choctaw and Chickasaw lands, oil and gas on the Creek and Cherokee territories. Since the children were completely ignorant about their holdings, the opportunities for graft and corruption were enormous.

Oklahoma judges regularly appointed guardians who had no interest in the children they were assigned to protect but were passionately interested in stealing their inheritances. They had dozens of illegal schemes. A common practice was selling a minor's land ostensibly for his or her benefit. When the land changed hands, 80 percent of the proceeds would be charged to court costs and attorneys' fees and the rest sidetracked into phony loans and investments. In reality, most of the funds went into the guardian's bank account.

Kate found one young man who owned oilfields so valuable that two different companies were fighting over the right to lease them. On the day before his twenty-first birthday, representatives of one of the companies enticed the youth into taking an automobile ride. Refusing to let him out of the car, they drove around all day and half the night. Finally, at one minute after midnight, when he officially came of age, they coerced him into signing the lease to the oilfields. By the time they returned the young man to his home, the document had already been witnessed by a notary public whom they had thoughtfully taken along on the ride.

On another occasion, a sixteen-year-old Indian boy was kidnapped and forced to marry a local prostitute. The marriage legally established his majority. The men who had staged the kidnapping then made him sign over the deed to his lands and had no trouble getting the transfer approved by the court.

Kate decided to undertake a probe of the orphans in Oklahoma's asylums. She discovered hundreds of Indian children who had been turned out to fend for themselves after their lands were taken from them by court-appointed guardians.

Infuriated by these injustices, Kate Barnard went before the state legislature and demanded that the Department of Charities and Corrections be given the right to intervene on behalf of any Indian whose estate was being mismanaged or handled dishonestly. She was concerned about adults as well as children. Many adult Indians could not read or write and did not understand business procedures. They were often cheated as badly as the children.

For the first time in her political life, Kate Barnard had a hard time mustering a majority. Some of the most respected men in the Oklahoma legislature were either profiting from the Indian land frauds or had powerful friends who were getting rich from them. After a ferocious battle, a feeble bill finally squeaked by. It did not give the Department of Charities and Corrections the sweeping powers that Kate had requested. The Department was restricted to overseeing the affairs of orphaned Indian minors.

Kate next tried to create an office of Public Defender to handle all the Indians' legal claims. Although the bill passed, it was vetoed by the Governor. Undaunted, Kate persuaded some of her friends on the budget committee to insert a special clause into the upcoming appropriations bill. The proviso increased the Department of Charities' allotment by $5,000 and specified that $2,500 of that was to be spent for legal services. Since the legislators could not vote against the clause without rejecting the entire state budget, Kate got her money.

She hired a lawyer named J. H. Stolper and told him to start investigating. Even Kate found it hard to believe what Stolper discovered. Almost every guardian had a half dozen children under his supposed supervision. Few made less than $15,000 from the fraudulent "sales" of their property. Soon, Stolper was prosecuting well over a hundred of those conscienceless guardians. Within a few months, he had his first conviction. The thief got five years in the penitentiary. Fourteen other guardians sweated under indictments involving misappropriations totaling $170,000. Other guardians rushed to return their stolen cash before the law got to them. In twelve months, Stolper recovered $949,390 for 1,361 Indian orphans.

A few Oklahomans were delighted with Kate's new program. Several judges who had long been concerned about the land frauds began quietly forwarding copies of guardians' reports to Kate's office, thus giving her attorney a head start in locating offenders. In Washington, a congressman from Oklahoma pointed with pride to Kate Barnard's crusade, calling her a "fearless defender of the weak and helpless."

Most Oklahomans, however, were not very enthusiastic about Stolper's work. Kate had told her attorney not to worry about politics or social standing. Democrats as well as Republicans, bankers as well as ordinary crooks were to be exposed and prosecuted. But as the probes continued and a number of influential men were implicated, Kate's popularity began to wane. The politicians held a secret meeting at which they agreed that something would have to be done about Kate Barnard. She was still much too popular to be attacked directly. Their plan was to destroy J. H. Stolper and put the legal office in the hands of one of their cronies.

When the Fourth Oklahoma Legislature met in 1912, a special committee searched the attorney's record for wrong-doing. They discovered a number of minor charges against Stolper and finally forced him out of office on the dubious grounds that he had used state funds to pay for trips to Washington and Boston to attend conferences on Indian affairs.

Kate said she would replace Stolper with an equally conscientious young lawyer. A group of legislators came to her and suggested that the man she had in mind did not have enough "experience" for the job. Perhaps she would consider a lawyer they had selected instead. Kate promised to think it over. But she recognized political blackmail when she saw it.

At that very moment there was a fight going on in the legislature over reducing the budget of the Department of Charities and Corrections. If Kate did not hire the attorney the legislative leaders wanted, her department would be wrecked. If she did hire him, she would have to abandon her efforts on behalf of the Indian children.

Kate spent several days fretting over her predicament. Then one morning she read in the *Daily Oklahoman* that the fight against her appropriation had been dropped and the Department of Charities and Corrections would be provided with ample funds. Assuming she had won another victory, Kate met with the legislative leaders and told them she was not going to hire their attorney. There was a moment of ominous silence. Then one of the men coldly informed Kate that the *Daily Oklahoman* had made a mistake. There was to be a second vote on the Department of Charities and Corrections budget.

A few weeks later, Kate found herself with no money to pay her staff. Her budget was reduced to zero. There was not enough cash left to pay for stationery or stamps. For the first time, Kate also found she was unable to tell her side of the story in the newspapers. Reporters avoided her. Privately, they told her an interview would be a waste of time. The publishers had joined the ugly conspiracy. They too had friends involved in the land frauds.

"Sympathy and sentiment never stand in the way of the onward march of empire," editorialized one paper. "If the Indians don't learn the value of property and how to adjust themselves to surroundings, they will be 'grafted' out of it—that is one of the unchangeable laws of God and the constitution of man."

Kate tried to keep her office open with $350 of her own money and a few hundred more borrowed from friends. Behind the scenes she fought desperately to get another vote on an emergency budget from the state legislature. But the men in charge of Oklahoma's politics had a handy slogan to frustrate her: economy. They talked about how the state budget had doubled in four years and hypocritically insisted the elimination of her appropriation was "necessary." Kate Barnard finally had to accept the bitter truth. Her Department of Charities and Corrections had ceased to exist. Her own words are the best description of what she saw and felt.

The dust collected in layers, and the spiders came and spun their webs in my silent, vacant department in which for years Christian men and women had devoted their whole time to raising standards of life for Oklahoma's poor. But the Fourth Legislature cut off their salaries and one by one these hospital inspectors, attorneys, inspectors of poorhouses, prisons, and jails departed—and left me alone. As I stood in the chill and gloom of my wrecked department I looked out of the State House window and noted that winter was dropping dead petals from the trees in the State House yard, and I thought how like these are the dead hopes and dreams which, chilled in the bitter wind of destiny, drop lifeless at our feet.

Kate Barnard's health had never been good. She suffered from chronic hay fever and her cool composure concealed an underlying emotional fragility that became more acute under stress. A disfiguring skin disease, probably psoriasis, began to torment her. But she continued her fight. Using the income from some property that her father had left her at his death in 1909 and the money she collected at fund-raising speeches—mostly quarters and half dollars from the workingmen who had been her earliest supporters— Kate organized a "People's Lobby." It had a dual purpose: to force the legislature to take a firm stand on Indian guardianships and to reinstate the Department of Charities and Corrections.

Aware of Kate's abilities as a leader, her political enemies tried to cajole her into silence. First, they offered her a chance to run for reelection to her old job with the guarantee that she would be unopposed. Refusing to be a party to any such deal, Kate replied with a decisive no. Next, there was a job opening in Washington at a salary of five thousand dollars a year. The only condition was that she stay out of Oklahoma politics. Again, Kate's answer was no. Instead, she threw herself into campaigning against two of the men who had conspired to wreck her department. One was defeated in the race for mayor of Muskogee, the

other lost his seat in Congress. But her lobby for Indian
rights was less successful. She haunted the Oklahoma legislature, distributing circulars whenever a bill to "rob Indians"
came up for a vote. Once she wangled permission to speak
on the Senate floor. She pleaded for a law protecting Indian
minors and condemned the senators who had voted against
such laws in the past. But nobody in Oklahoma—or in the
rest of the country—seemed to care what was happening to
the Indians. The bills for which Kate lobbied were invariably defeated, the newspapers remained hostile to her,
and the federal government remained deaf to her appeals
for a congressional investigation of the land scandals. The
nation was smugly convinced that "progress" was taking care
of the Indians.

For the next twenty years Kate continued to speak
out for the Indians, but it was not an issue on which she
could rebuild her shattered political career. She became
more and more harassed by her skin disease, and a general
nervous exhaustion which today we would probably call
depression. She died in 1930 at the age of fifty-five, a defeated, forgotten name in Oklahoma. Two histories of the
state, both published by the University of Oklahoma, do not
even mention her name. They also fail to mention anything
about Oklahomans robbing the Indians.

Kate Barnard died thinking of herself as a failure.
But like Prudence Crandall, the cause for which she fought
did not die. In 1926, a growing chorus of critics persuaded
the government to fund a study by the Brookings Institution
to see how the Indians were faring under the land allotment system. The findings, published in 1928 and confirmed
by a long, thorough congressional investigation, stunned the
nation. Poverty, starvation, humiliation, had become a way
of life for tens of thousands of Indians. In 1887, they had
owned 138,000,000 acres of land. By 1934, their holdings

had shrunk to 47,000,000. In Oklahoma, the land belonging to the five largest tribes had dwindled from 19,500,000 acres to 1,500,000. In 1948, when my father asked former President Herbert Hoover to reorganize the Executive Department of the federal government, the two Presidents concurred in a bipartisan condemnation of the allotment policy. "The rationalization behind this policy is so obviously false that it could not have prevailed for so long a time if not supported by the avid demands for Indian lands. This was a way of getting them at bargain prices."

By that time, Congress had formally abandoned the allotment system and set up a government loan program which permitted thousands of Indians to buy back 400,000 acres of farmland and 7,000,000 acres of grazing land that they had lost. Thousands of Indian families are living on this land today, prosperous, self-supporting citizens of the United States.

I wish I could say that all the injustices that Kate Barnard fought have been rectified. But this is an imperfect world. At least, her gallant voice, ignored in her own time, was heard by courageous men and women of another era. It is one more example of a woman of courage transcending the limitations of her time and place.

"I Speak As a Woman"

The United States Senate is sometimes referred to as the world's most exclusive men's club. Over the years, only a few women have found their way into its hallowed chamber. Three were appointed by Governors to finish out unexpired terms. A fourth, Hattie Caraway of Arkansas, served out the unexpired term of her deceased husband and was reelected on her own in 1932 and 1938.

Senator Caraway was the creature of local political bosses and spent much of her time in the Senate knitting and doing crossword puzzles. Her only political interest was in trying, without success, to get a law passed that would require airlines to issue parachutes to their passengers. Otherwise she said and did practically nothing. "I haven't the heart to take a minute from the men," she once said. "The poor dears love it so."

The next woman to be elected to the United States Senate resembled Hattie Caraway about as much as a Maine winter resembles an Arkansas summer. Margaret Chase Smith was a slim, silver-haired, professional politician whose credentials were as good or better than those of most of her male colleagues. A native of Skowhegan, Maine, Margaret Chase had gone to work as a telephone operator soon after her graduation from high school. She was quickly promoted to a position in the business office, went on to become circulation manager of Skowhegan's weekly newspaper, and then stepped into an even better job as office manager of the local woolen mill. By the time she married Clyde Smith in 1930, Margaret was one of the most successful young businesswomen in the state of Maine.

Smith, who was then a state senator, was a skilled politician and one of the best vote-getters in Maine's Republican party. His thirty-three-year-old bride soon became as thoroughly versed in politics as her husband. When Clyde Smith was elected to Congress from Maine's Second District in 1936, Margaret, who had long been his unofficial secretary, took the job on an official basis. Besides running the office and answering the mail, she did research on the bills her husband would be voting on and traveled with him on fact-finding tours for his work on the House Labor Committee.

When Clyde Smith died of a heart attack in 1940, it seemed the most natural thing in the world for his partner in public as well as private life to become a candidate for his seat. Reelected four times on her own, she decided to run for the Senate in 1948 against almost unanimous opposition from Maine's Republican party bosses. To win the nomination, she had had to beat two of the state's best Republican vote-getters in the primary. In the fall of 1948, she went on to thrash her Democratic opponent with 71 percent of the vote. The coattails of the Democratic candidate for President that year, Harry S. Truman, did not reach to Maine, thank goodness.

Throughout her career in Congress, Margaret Chase Smith had her own highly personal style. She tended to be taciturn, like most down-easters. She never ran off at the mouth and she was not especially fond of people who had this tendency. She preferred to work behind the scenes, on

WIDE WORLD PHOTOS

Margaret Chase Smith doing what comes naturally to her: campaigning. This was one of her many talents that Senator Joseph McCarthy badly underestimated.

the committees where the real business of Congress is done, and let others do the orating on the House or Senate floor. When she made a speech, it was to say something important.

This did not mean that her male colleagues always listened to her. In fact, one of Senator Smith's most important speeches went largely unheard and ignored when she gave it and has since been all but forgotten. But I believe it was one of the most dramatic moments in the history of the United States Senate. For what she said—and what she risked to say it—Margaret Chase Smith deserves to be ranked among the gallant women.

If you were alive and old enough to be reading the newspapers during the period that historians now refer to as "the Truman era," you will remember that one of the hottest issues of the day was communism and, more particularly, Communist subversion in the United States Government.

It was not a new issue. Conservatives had been fulminating about Communists and communism in Franklin D. Roosevelt's New Deal throughout the thirties. The FBI had been vigorously investigating the possibility of Communist influence in the federal government since 1945, when our World War II honeymoon with Soviet Russia was coming to a bitter end. A handful of minor officials who were either Communists or had links to Communists had been uncovered. But in 1948, a self-confessed former courier for a Soviet spy ring, Whittaker Chambers, made headlines with claims of far more serious Communist penetration.

Chambers singled out Alger Hiss, a top-level State Department official who had been on President Roosevelt's staff at Yalta and who had since left the government to become head of the Carnegie Endowment for International Peace. When Hiss denied Chambers's charges under oath, his accuser produced a startling number of documents which he claimed to have received from Hiss during the late 1930s. Tried for perjury, Hiss was convicted on January 25, 1950.

Thirteen days later, the British government arrested a German-born physicist, Klaus Fuchs, and accused him of stealing atomic secrets and passing them to the Russians. Earlier, my father had warned the American public that the Soviet Union possessed the theoretical knowledge to make the bomb, and it was only a question of time before they did so. But it was still a shock to discover that the Russians had accelerated their schedule and worse, that they had done so with the help of a spy ring. Add to these shocks the cries of alarm being raised by those who blamed the American government for "losing" the Republic of China to Mao Tse-tung's Communists, and the stage was set for the entrance of a man who ultimately became one of the most dangerous politicians in America—Senator Joseph McCarthy.

McCarthy had spent four years in the U. S. Senate without showing any interest in the Communists-in-government issue. But he was up for reelection in 1952 and he needed something to arouse the voters of Wisconsin, who were showing alarming signs of becoming apathetic about their do-nothing junior senator.

On February 9, 1950, McCarthy made a speech to the Republican Women's Club of Wheeling, West Virginia, in which he announced that there were 206 Communists employed by the Department of State and that my father's Secretary of State, Dean Acheson, was protecting them. McCarthy had compiled his speech from a patchwork of sources and embellished them at will. If anyone had been able to check the facts against these sources, McCarthy would have been discredited overnight. But he clutched his "confidential" information to his brawny chest and refused to let anyone examine it.

The day after the Wheeling speech, Klaus Fuchs made

a full confession of his espionage activities to British authorities. Within a few months the FBI had closed in on American confederates who had helped him smuggle atomic secrets to Russia—David Greenglass, Morton Sobel, Harry Gold, Julius and Ethel Rosenberg. McCarthy gleefully seized on this revelation as proof that Communists infested our government. He added to the hysteria with additional speeches in Reno and Salt Lake City and returned to Washington to stage a blazing eight-hour session on the floor of the Senate in which he painted a frightening picture of pro-Communist infiltrators—"twisted-minded intellectuals" he called them—trying to take over both political parties.

Headlines blossomed in newspapers across the country, and before long, a Senate committee headed by Democrat Millard Tydings of Maryland was organized to investigate McCarthy's charges. But the Democrats made a dreadful mistake. They decided that Joe McCarthy was not worth being taken seriously. The Tydings Committee treated him with complete contempt when he appeared before them on March 8, 1950. One writer described the scene as "an unequal contest between an enraged hick and an accomplished city slicker, with the latter, in the person of Tydings, getting the applause and the laughs."

When the Democrats on the committee demanded that McCarthy provide the names of his contacts in the State Department who were giving him information about security risks, it was McCarthy's turn to score. "You are not fooling me!" he roared. "You want the information so that heads will fall in the State Department!"

The Tydings Committee also made the mistake of insisting that McCarthy identify disloyal members of the State Department in public session, thus giving him a chance to smear distinguished diplomats like Philip Jessup and John Stewart Service for their "Communist affiliations." The

State Department instantly rushed into print with a statement affirming the integrity of Service and Jessup, again playing into McCarthy's hands. He fulminated that their "whitewash" proved the striped-pants bureaucrats had no real interest in investigating his charges.

Senator McCarthy was unable to prove his case against a single person he named. He was feeding on the fear created by the Hiss conviction and the atomic spy-ring revelations. But that fear was widespread enough to win him a substantial following. Anti-Communist fanatics hounded the people he accused of being Communists or fellow travelers with threatening phone calls and harassed their wives and children. The threats continued even after government investigators had cleared their names. Men who had spent decades building reputations for integrity saw themselves ruined by a single swipe of McCarthy's tarbrush. Many were fired for unexplained reasons and were unable to get jobs anywhere. Guilty or innocent, they had become instant pariahs.

But the leaders of the Republican party paid more attention to McCarthy's growing number of followers. These multiplied dramatically, thanks to another Democratic blunder. Senator Dennis Chavez of New Mexico attacked McCarthy and announced that he was speaking "not only as an American but as a Catholic." Millions of Catholics— particularly Irish Americans—got mad enough to join Joe's phony crusade. When my father, speaking much more to the point, called McCarthy "the Kremlin's greatest asset," the Republican party's leading spokesman, Senator Robert Taft of Ohio, leaped to his defense. He accused the President of libeling the senator from Wisconsin.

But there was one member of the Republican party who did not share this steadily growing enthusiasm for Joe McCarthy. Margaret Chase Smith had been sworn in for her first term in the United States Senate in January, 1949. At the time, she made a point of the fact that she was there as a United States senator and not as a woman. "I consider that women are people," she said, "and the record they make is a matter of ability and desire rather than of their sex."

Unquestionably, this was sound thinking and good politics. But I am convinced that being a woman had a lot to do with her lack of enthusiasm for Senator McCarthy—and even more with her decision to say something about it. McCarthy's smear-on-the-run tactics threatened those fundamental feelings of mutual trust and decency on which our sense of community depends. Women are inclined to be more sensitive to these feelings than men—and to react more angrily to their violation.

Margaret Chase Smith had been studying Senator McCarthy closely since his Wheeling speech, and she did not like what she saw and heard. He still refused to let anyone, even fellow Republican senators, examine the list of Communists, the "proof" which he flourished so dramatically in his speeches. Once Senator Smith had asked to see a document, and McCarthy had replied: "What's the matter, Margaret, don't you trust me?"

As far as Senator Smith could see, McCarthy's main interest was making headlines. He was also a genius at capitalizing on the enormous turbulence he created with still more reckless charges. Senator Smith noted that McCarthy usually made his accusations on the Senate floor, where congressional immunity prevented his victims from suing him for libel.

What was even more distressing, Senator McCarthy was also becoming a formidable political power. As his followers multiplied, his tactics became more ruthless and immoral. Two fellow senators who had incurred his wrath,

Claude Pepper of Florida and Frank Graham of North Carolina, went down to defeat in primary contests that featured McCarthy-style charges of Communist leanings. Anyone who opposed him could expect a similar no-holds-barred counterattack.

Watching this sordid show, which had brought all business in the Senate to a standstill, Margaret Chase Smith became more and more uneasy. She tried at first to suppress her doubts. She was hoping that McCarthy would stop making inflammatory speeches and produce some solid evidence. As a Republican, she could see that his charges, if they were true, would guarantee a GOP victory in the next election.

As the accusations increased and still no evidence was forthcoming, Senator Smith began to lose her patience. She abhorred the atmosphere of repression and fear that Joe McCarthy was creating in the country. It even extended into the United States Senate. Lawmakers hesitated to talk to, or even be seen with, fellow lawmakers who might be on McCarthy's list of Communist sympathizers. They lived in dread of being attacked on the Senate floor. It was next to impossible to reply to a McCarthy-style barrage. Some courageous Democratic senators, such as William Benton of Connecticut, did try to answer him. But by this time, McCarthy was able to dismiss anything from the Democratic side of the aisle as biased and partisan.

From the Republican side of the aisle came only silence, or covert whispers of support, and even some cautious applause. Senator Taft said that Senator McCarthy should keep up the good work, and if one case did not uncover a Communist conspiracy, he should drop it and try another one on his list. This seemed to Senator Taft a good formula for making the Democrats look worse every day. But Mar-

garet Chase Smith found herself wondering if McCarthyism
was too high a price even for victory-starved Republicans to
pay.

One day in the late spring of 1950, she sat at her desk
in the Senate chamber and listened while Joe McCarthy
smeared the reputations of some half dozen defenseless
Americans. When several Democratic senators rose to stop
him, they were met with a merciless tirade of insults and
accusations.

Senator Smith returned to her office, bristling with
rage. She described the scene she had just witnessed to her
chief administrative assistant William Lewis. "Bill," she said,
in a voice choked with anger, "I just don't know why someone from our party doesn't speak out against that man!"

"Have you thought of doing it yourself?" Lewis replied quietly.

Senator Smith shook her head. She had been in the
United States Senate a little over a year, and so far she had
spoken only once. That was on February 22 when, at the
request of Vice-President Alben W. Barkley, she had continued the old Senate custom of reading Washington's Fare-
well Address. Contributing to her natural Yankee taciturnity
was the Senate tradition that freshmen solons did not make
speeches during their first months in office. This made sense
to Senator Smith. She had always believed that people should
listen and "get their feet placed" before they spoke out. Besides, if anyone was going to rebuke the Republican party's
hottest celebrity, it should be a senior senator or a party
spokesman like Robert Taft or William Knowland of California.

During the next week, watching the deference with
which these gentlemen greeted Senator McCarthy, the attention they lavished on him, Senator Smith slowly realized that
no male member of the club was ever going to cross the

junior senator from Wisconsin. If she wanted to hear an indictment of him on the Republican side of the aisle, it would have to come from her own lips.

Margaret Chase Smith knew that her voice alone would not carry the impact that the situation demanded. She called her old friend and fellow New Englander Senator George Aiken of Vermont and asked him to join her. Her plan was to present a brief but pointed objection to the GOP's silent acquiescence to Senator McCarthy's behavior. She called it a Declaration of Conscience.

Aiken assured her of his support. So did the five other Republicans she approached—a carefully selected cross-section of the Senate that included Robert Hendrickson of New Jersey, Irving Ives of New York, Wayne Morse of Oregon (who later became a Democrat), Edward Thye of Minnesota, and Charles Tobey of New Hampshire.

The Declaration of Conscience was concerned mainly with party politics. It contained some hard knocks against the Democrats, but it also reminded both parties that they ought to stop thinking about elections and start thinking about national security based on a policy of individual freedom. "It is high time," it said, "that we all stopped being tools or victims of totalitarian techniques—techniques that, if continued unchecked, will surely end what we have come to cherish in the American way of life."

There were sterner things aimed even more directly at Senator McCarthy that Margaret Chase Smith might have added if she felt she had enough authority to present the Declaration all by herself. They were on her mind when she went back to Maine for the Memorial Day recess. She spent the entire journey talking to her chief administrative assistant about the kind of speech that ought to be made against Senator Joseph McCarthy. By the time she got to her home in Skowhegan, she had gone so far as to make a rough draft of the things she wanted to say. She passed it along to Bill Lewis, who fashioned it into a formal speech.

Margaret Chase Smith could have found few places more appropriate than Skowhegan, Maine, to set down her thoughts about freedom in the United States. New Englanders have never been noted for their free-wheeling attitudes toward life, but there is, at the core of the Yankee character, a profound respect for individual liberty. It was this search for one important liberty—the freedom to worship as they pleased —that brought the first settlers to the rugged shores of Massachusetts. This same love of liberty inspired New Englanders to lead America's revolt against Great Britain's reactionary rule one hundred and fifty years later.

Senator Smith had said nothing to her fellow signers of the Declaration about a speech. "To be honest with you," she told me when I visited her recently, "I was a little doubtful if I would be able to carry through on it. That was how nervous I was about it."

Anyone with a little knowledge of Washington politics can understand why she was nervous. It takes tremendous courage to buck the most powerful men in your own political party. When the power struggle takes place in the U. S. Senate, the voltage is really frightening. Senator Smith was a veteran politician. She knew what these party leaders could do to her. They could deprive her of the chance to serve on important committees. They could make sure that she was not invited to speak at party dinners. They could deny her many of the perquisites—the right to approve federal appointees from Maine, for instance—that she needed to win reelection. Giving the speech would endanger her career as a politician. It would also bring certain revenge from the wrathful senator from Wisconsin.

But the prospect of political ostracism was not quite

as frightening to Margaret Chase Smith as it might have been to one of her male colleagues. She had already defied Maine's Republican bosses when they had objected to giving the senatorial nomination to a woman. In the Senate, she remained fiercely independent, feeling little obligation to defer to male politicians who sometimes excluded her from high-level gatherings by holding them at Washington, D.C.'s "men only" clubs.

By the time Margaret Chase Smith returned to the capital after the Memorial Day recess, she had in her brief-case a neatly typed speech. No one except Bill Lewis knew of its existence, and Senator Smith tried hard to keep it a secret, too. She asked Lewis to mimeograph the speech himself and told him not to distribute any copies to the press until she was on her feet at least three minutes. "I may not be able to go through with this, Bill," she said. "This is a pretty difficult thing."

Bill Lewis knew his senator. "You'll be all right," he said.

On June 1, 1950, Margaret Chase Smith and Bill Lewis boarded the small underground train that carries passengers between the Senate Office Building and the Capitol. A few seconds later, who should step on and sit down beside them but the burly senator from Wisconsin. Margaret gave him a perfunctory nod and then stared straight ahead.

The senator from Wisconsin could not help remarking on her solemn mood. "Margaret," he said, "you look like you've got something on your mind."

"Yes, Joe, I have," she replied. "I think I'm going to make a speech and I don't think you're going to like it."

McCarthy just grinned. He was riding too high to be bothered by criticism, especially from a woman who barely came up to his shoulder.

"Just remember," he said, wagging his finger under her nose, "I can see to it that you don't get any of Wisconsin's votes for the vice-presidency."

There had been some talk among the Republicans of nominating Margaret Chase Smith for Vice-President in the upcoming 1952 elections. In the not too distant future, she would become the first serious woman candidate for the presidential nomination. But she had no interest in the vice-presidency. McCarthy's threat was meaningless.

In the Senate Chamber, Margaret Chase Smith indicated to Vice-President Alben Barkley that she wanted to take the floor. Bill Lewis had already spoken to the Vice-President, and he had agreed to recognize her promptly. Lewis stood against the wall of the chamber, a few feet away, the mimeographed speeches rolled under his arm. He was obeying his boss's order to wait until she talked for three minutes before going upstairs to the gallery to distribute copies to the press.

The gallery was crowded. Rumors had been circulating around Washington all week that Senator Smith was finally going to make a major speech. Almost all the senators were also at their desks—a comparative rarity. Senator McCarthy, a confident smile on his face, was sitting immediately behind Senator Smith.

"I would like to speak briefly and simply about a serious national condition," she began. "There is a national feeling of fear and frustration that can result in national suicide and the end of everything that we hold dear."

Glancing coolly at Senator McCarthy, she reminded her listeners that the United States Senate "has long enjoyed worldwide respect as the greatest deliberative body in the world. But recently that deliberative character has too often been debased to a forum of hate and character assassination, sheltered by the shield of congressional immunity. It is ironic that we senators can in debate in the Senate impute to any American who is not a senator any conduct unworthy or unbecoming an American—and without that nonsenator American having any legal redress against us. Yet if we say the same thing in the Senate about our colleagues, we can be stopped on the grounds of being out of order."

At this point, Republican senators began walking out in droves. Soon, almost the only Republicans on the floor were the six senators who had pledged to support her Declaration of Conscience. The departing Republicans were joined, I regret to report, by a number of Democrats. But Senator McCarthy did not move from his seat. He sat there, glowering ominously at Senator Smith's back, waiting to see what she would do when confronted with this mass exodus.

Out of the corner of her eye, Senator Smith saw Bill Lewis leaving the chamber for the press gallery with the copies of the speech. In a matter of seconds he would be handing them out to the press. It was too late to stop now. But she had no intention of stopping and continued in a clear, unwavering voice.

"I speak as a Republican. I speak as a woman. I speak as a United States senator. I speak as an American. I think it is high time that we remember that we have sworn to uphold and defend the Constitution. I think it is high time that we remember that the Constitution as amended speaks not only of the freedom of speech but also of trial by jury, not trial by accusation.

"Those of us who shout the loudest about Americanism in making character assassinations," she went on, "are all too frequently those who by our own words and acts ignore some of the basic principles of Americanism:

"The right to criticize,

"The right to hold unpopular beliefs,

"The right to protest,

"The right to independent thought."

There was more to the speech, including an attack on the Truman Administration, but it ended with some harsh words for the members of her own party who were encouraging Senator McCarthy because he was such an excellent weapon against the Democrats. "I don't want to see the Republican party ride to political victory on the four horsemen of calumny—fear, ignorance, bigotry, and smear," she said. "I don't want to see the Republican party win that way. Though it might be a fleeting victory for the Republican party, it would be a more lasting defeat for the American people."

Senator Smith concluded by reading the Declaration of Conscience signed by herself and the other six Republican senators.

By this time, Senator Joseph McCarthy was white-faced and grim. As Margaret Chase Smith's last words rang through the chamber, one newspaperman said he felt that "a much-needed breath of fresh air" had penetrated the Capitol at last. For Senator McCarthy, it was more like an uppercut to the jaw. He had no ready retort to this forthright woman in her trim silk suit. Scowling, he strode up the aisle and disappeared into the cloakroom without a word.

The next day, McCarthy's answer appeared in the newspapers. He contemptuously dismissed the speech and the declaration as nonsense from "Snow White and her Six Dwarfs." This was only the beginning of his revenge. When the next session of Congress met, Senator Smith, without a word of warning, was ousted from her seat on the Senate Permanent Investigating Committee and replaced by a new Republican senator from California, Richard M. Nixon.

As the ranking Republican on the committee, McCarthy had the power to eliminate her, but it was unprecedented to do such a thing. Once named to a committee, a senator customarily remains there until he or she decides to retire or resign. Although Senator Smith protested vigorously to the Democratic chairman of the committee, he declined to intervene. Like everyone else, he did not want to tangle with Joe McCarthy.

Senator McCarthy next began telling people that he was going to "break" Margaret Chase Smith "politically, mentally, and financially." He tried to make good on these threats in 1954 when he persuaded a native of Maine who had worked with him on the Senate Investigating Committee to oppose Senator Smith in the Republican primary. McCarthy gave his man a sweeping endorsement and denounced Senator Smith as a friend of Communists and fellow travelers.

McCarthy's man had oil money from Texas behind him, and he spent it lavishly. Even if he did not defeat Senator Smith, McCarthy hoped that he would force her to spend so much money in the primary that she would have nothing left to finance her election campaign.

But Senator McCarthy soon discovered that he was dealing with a very special politician. Mrs. Smith did not accept large political contributions, and she spent practically no money on her campaigns. She knew the people of Maine would not be impressed by splashy publicity. Her primary campaign consisted of traveling by car or train to practically every city, town, and village in the state to tell people what she had done for them and ask them for their votes. She beat McCarthy's candidate, five to one.

By this time the Republican members of the Senate realized that they should have listened to Margaret Chase Smith. Joe McCarthy was smearing the Republican tenant in the White House, Dwight D. Eisenhower, as viciously as he had previously attacked Harry S. Truman. In the intervening years, McCarthy's power had grown to terrifying proportions. He had continued his havoc at the polls, helping to defeat Millard Tydings in Maryland and Scott Lucas, the

Senate majority leader, in Illinois. He had, in addition, demoralized the State Department, practically dismembered the U. S. Information Agency, and blatantly interfered in the conduct of American foreign policy. Only when McCarthy tried to extend his power to the U. S. Army did President Eisenhower attempt to rally Senate Republicans against him.

Senator Ralph Flanders of Vermont introduced a motion to censure McCarthy. The fact that a "mere woman"—as Senator Smith wryly described herself—had proven in the Maine primary that McCarthy could be beaten had not a little to do with persuading the Senate to take Flanders's motion seriously. The powerful lobby organized by the National Committee for an Effective Congress also played a major role in the tortuous process by which Senate Republicans finally joined Democrats to vote to censure McCarthy and finish him politically.

Being stiffnecked males, the Republicans never admitted that the senator from Maine had been right from the start. They left it to a Democrat, Senator Stuart Symington of Missouri, to produce my favorite description of Margaret Chase Smith. "She represents just about all that is best today in American public life," he said. "Even if she is a Republican."

The Doctor Who Said No

Kate Barnard and Margaret Chase Smith fought their battles on public stages. Although they did not win instant victories, there was always the hope that enough consciences had been stirred to make vindication possible at some future date.

Frances Oldham Kelsey had no such consolation. Her fight took place entirely within the paint-peeling halls and dingy offices of a government agency—the Food and Drug Administration. There were no legislators to cajole, no public to reach, not even a group of grievously wronged children or adults to whom she could point. She fought to protect infants who did not yet exist.

Dr. Frances Oldham first attracted attention in the scientific world in 1943 when she and a fellow pharmacologist, Dr. Fremont Ellis Kelsey, reported some highly creative laboratory work about the effect of certain drugs on unborn rabbits.

Born in Vancouver, the daughter of a retired British army officer, "Frankie" Oldham had always wanted to be a scientist. She acquired bachelor and master of science degrees at McGill University in Montreal, and a Ph.D. from the University of Chicago in 1938. At Chicago, she worked

with one of the great scientists of our era, Dr. E. M. K. Geiling, a founder of a new branch of medicine, pharmacology.
The study of the effect of drugs on the body, pharmacology was in its infancy or, at best, childhood, in those days.
Geiling communicated to the young woman scientist a vivid
sense of its importance in the medical world. He also gave
her his passion for scrupulously high standards of research.

Geiling warmly praised the results of Dr. Oldham and
Dr. Kelsey's rabbit experiments and helped to get them published. The researchers noted that the liver of an adult female
rabbit was normally able to absorb a drug such as quinine
rapidly because of the presence of an enzyme. But quinine
was a deadly drug to the fetus in the same rabbit's womb,
because the liver of an unborn rabbit did not develop this
enzyme until after birth. Frances Oldham and Fremont Kelsey were among the first scientists to call attention to the fact
that some drugs which adults can take safely can be dangerous
to embryos in the womb.

At the end of 1943, this research produced another
important result. Drs. Oldham and Kelsey were married,
proving that for some people, the laboratory can be as ro-
mantic as a rose garden.

A few years later, Frances Kelsey decided an M.D.
degree might add to her pharmacologist's expertise. She obtained one at the University of Chicago medical school, un-
bothered by the birth of two daughters during the four-year
course. After a few more years of joint teaching and research
on that university's faculty and a similar stint at the University of South Dakota, Dr. Fremont Kelsey accepted a job
with the Division of General Medical Sciences at the National Institutes of Health. Frances Kelsey and her two
daughters moved with him to Washington. There she was
offered a job in the Food and Drug Administration as a

WIDE WORLD PHOTOS

Dr. Frances O. Kelsey wears the Distinguished Federal Civilian Service Medal which she received from President Kennedy on Aug. 7, 1962, for her refusal to permit the sale of the drug thalidomide in America.

medical officer. Her responsibility: to evaluate applications for licenses to market new drugs.

Frances Kelsey did not realize it, but she was walking into a federal agency honeycombed with dissension and conflict. A major investigation of the drug industry and its relationship to the agency was being conducted by a Senate Committee headed by Estes Kefauver of Tennessee. A top official of the agency had been accused of taking more than a quarter of a million dollars in private fees from drug companies for working as an editor of journals promoting the very drugs he was supposed to be licensing. More startling was Dr. Kelsey's discovery that the woman doctor who had preceded her in the New Drug Section of the FDA, Dr. Barbara Moulton, had quit in disgust because her superiors had repeatedly overruled her decisions.

Shortly after Dr. Kelsey went to work at the FDA, Dr. Moulton appeared as a witness before the Kefauver committee and denounced the way the FDA was operating. She was particularly critical of the close relationships between FDA officials and drug makers and the way agents of the drug companies were permitted to harass FDA doctors and scientists with constant phone calls and visits. Sitting in the audience while Dr. Moulton testified was Dr. Frances O. Kelsey. She introduced herself to her predecessor after the testimony, and the two became close friends. This in itself was an act of considerable courage. Hardly anyone in Washington outside the Kefauver committee was talking to Dr. Moulton at this point. Inside the Food and Drug Administration her unpopularity was monumental.

Meanwhile, Dr. Kelsey was learning the realities of life within the New Drug Section. Her office was an uncarpeted cubicle in a rickety barracks that the government had built during World War II for temporary use. There were blinds but no curtains on the windows. Faded green paint peeled from the walls. In an average year the drug companies presented 693 applications for new medicines, 282 of them for human use (the rest were veterinarian drugs). The twelve chemists, twelve doctors, and handful of pharmacologists in the New Drug Section had sixty days to review each one of these drugs. Unless they could find some scientific reason to fault the applications, the manufacturer had the right to put the drug on the market.

If the FDA scientists found a legitimate objection, they had to send a written letter to the manufacturer within that sixty-day period, requesting a new submission. This would extend their time to study the drug another sixty days, during which period the company would try to answer their objections. It was a bizarre situation. The pressure was on the overworked FDA officials to find something wrong. The momentum was all on the side of the drug companies with their lavish brochures, ample staffs, and fat profits. Moreover, there was no provision in the law to prevent drug companies from "testing" new medicines on startling numbers of Americans before applying for a license to market the drug.

On September 12, 1960, only a few months after Frances Kelsey had joined the FDA, the William S. Merrell Company, a 134-year-old pharmaceutical concern from Cincinnati, Ohio, applied for a license to market a new drug called Kevadon. It was a sleeping pill, and the application noted that it had been sold to millions of consumers in West Germany, where it was first developed, and in eleven other European nations, seven African, seventeen Asiatic, and eleven Western Hemisphere countries, including Canada. It had various trade names—Contergan in Germany, Distaval in England. In liquid form, it seemed to relieve the nausea of early pregnancy and was given to millions of expectant mothers. Basically, the drug was a sedative. In England, it was called "the sleeping pill of the century." It appeared to provide a deep, natural sleep without any of the hangovers, the drained, drugged feelings caused by barbiturates. Would-be suicides who swallowed dozens of them recovered. Best of all, it was cheap.

The drug which these various names confused and concealed was thalidomide. It was first synthesized by a Swiss pharmaceutical house in 1954. The Swiss company abandoned the drug when it showed no effects on laboratory animals. A West German drug firm, Chemie Grünenthal, tried it on epileptics and noticed that while it did not prevent convulsions, it was an excellent sleeping pill. By the early 1960s, thalidomide accounted for 46 percent of Grünenthal's gross profits.

The Merrell Company obviously looked forward to similar success with the drug in the United States. During the fall of 1960, while Dr. Kelsey was studying their application, Merrell issued a manual to its employees telling them how to distribute the two thousand kilograms of thalidomide the firm had imported from Grünenthal. Under the drug law in force at that time, a company could distribute a dangerously large amount of a drug even before the FDA approved it, as long as they labeled it experimental. Merrell told their salesmen "to contact teaching hospitals . . . and the chief and senior members of the departments of surgery, medicine, anesthesiology, and obstetrics/gynecology, for the purpose of selling them Kevadon and providing them with a clinical supply." The goal was not only to "accumulate a series of clinical reports on Kevadon's indications" but also "to perfect and develop the best possible detailed story for a national introduction of Kevadon."

How little interest Merrell had in research was visible in another part of the manual. They told their salesmen to "bear in mind that these are not *basic* clinical research studies. We have firmly established the safety, dosage, and usefulness of Kevadon by both foreign and U. S. laboratory clinical studies. This program is designed to gain more widespread *confirmation* of its usefulness in a variety of hospitalized patients. . . . The main purpose is to establish local studies whose results will be spread among hospital staff members. You can assure your doctors that they need not report results if they don't want to but that we, naturally, would like to know of their results. Be sure to tell them that we may send them report forms or reminder letters, but these are strictly reminders and they need not reply. . . . Appeal to the doctor's ego—we think he is important enough to be selected as one of the first to use Kevadon in that section of the country."

In Germany and England, even scarier things were happening while Dr. Kelsey studied Merrell's application. Chemie Grünenthal's claim that the drug was "nontoxic," "completely harmless even for infants," "harmless even over a long period of use," were being challenged by a growing number of doctors. After using thalidomide for as little as two weeks, some people began to have prickling sensations in their hands and feet, followed by numbness and coldness. The numbness spread from the toes to the ball of the foot and, in some cases, up the calves to the knees. A similar numbness enveloped the hands and moved up the arms. Then came severe muscular pains and cramps, followed by an unbalanced, uncoordinated walk. The medical term for this condition is polyneuritis. Often the victims became permanently disabled. Other signs that thalidomide damaged the nervous system of humans also appeared: twitching muscles in the face, trembling muscles throughout the body, inability to concentrate, speech difficulties, and double vision. These symptoms usually ceased when the person stopped using thalidomide. But in some 20 percent of the cases, the polyneuritis in the hands and feet did not reverse itself.

Grünenthal's response to these alarming reports was a violent publicity campaign reaffirming the drug's safety. One salesman wrote, "My happy laughter and appropriate references to the harmless properties of the drug were apparently successful in putting the often anxious pharmacists' minds at rest." The company arranged for tests in public asylums on patients who were not likely to give accurate reports of their reactions to thalidomide or any other drug.

In Washington, Dr. Kelsey and her pharmacologist-chemist team were evaluating the scientific data supplied by the William Merrell Company in their application. As required by law, the company had conducted experiments with the drug on animals and reported no evidence of toxicity. But these studies revealed an oddity—thalidomide did not make animals sleepy. This suggested to Dr. Kelsey that the drug was much more complex than Merrell said it was. Both the chemist and the pharmacologist working with her found the data submitted by Merrell incomplete. Dr. Kelsey was even more dissatisfied with the reports of the effects on humans. "The clinical work was not well documented," she told me in a recent interview. "Many of the studies were done elsewhere—mostly in Europe. The animal studies were also incomplete."

On November 10, 1960, two days before the sixty-day automatic approval period expired, Dr. Kelsey advised Merrell that she considered their application "inadequate" and asked for new data. Within the next few weeks Merrell submitted some new data, and Dr. F. Joseph Murray, executive assistant to the Merrell director of research, called on Dr. Kelsey, bringing with him another Merrell representative and further data. The two Merrell men could not understand why Dr. Kelsey had any doubts about Kevadon. Dr.

Kelsey told them she was worried about the drug's toxicity. Since humans were fifty times as sensitive as animals to the sedative effect of Kevadon, humans might also be sensitive in much more negative ways that were not being detected in animal experiments. The low toxicity about which Merrell and the German and British drug companies were constantly boasting might be explained by poor absorption in the gastrointestinal tract. None of the data given by Merrell told how the drug was absorbed and distributed by the body. If it was poorly absorbed, it might concentrate in one part of the body and be very damaging.

The Merrell men pooh-poohed all this sound pharmacological reasoning. On December 28, Dr. Murray was back with more data and more argument. When Dr. Kelsey went through this new material, she noticed that it was not in duplicate, which was required by a government regulation. She called Dr. Murray to point this out, and he told her it was just for her "personal information" and he saw no need to include it in the application. In her quiet, unassuming way, Dr. Kelsey told Murray that she could not accept scientific information on an off-the-record basis. She saw that he was treating her like an unreasonable female, humoring her with this extra information and at the same time insulting her by implying that the material in the application was already more than sufficient to win FDA approval. The conversation ended with Dr. Murray urging her to meet with him soon. Merrell was in a hurry to prepare for marketing the drug.

On January 9, 1961, Dr. Murray was on the telephone to Dr. Kelsey requesting a meeting to discuss the label for the drug. On the eleventh of January, Murray delivered more data to Dr. Kelsey and on the seventeenth submitted a letter with suggestions for a label. He asked Dr. Kelsey to telephone him if it was satisfactory so Merrell could proceed with "its marketing arrangements." Dr. Kelsey's reply was another official letter requesting Merrell to withdraw the application and resubmit it for another sixty-day period.

Eight days later, Murray was on the telephone to Dr. Ralph Smith, Dr. Kelsey's immediate superior in the agency, complaining because Dr. Kelsey had not been available for one of his telephone calls. Murray told Smith that Merrell was waiting to print the drug labels and—implying that Dr. Kelsey was playing the role of an oddball obstructionist— maintained that the "wording of the labels" was the only point remaining to be clarified. Dr. Smith promised to investigate the matter.

For those who know anything about office politics, Dr. Murray's move was a classic gambit. He had gone over Dr. Kelsey's head to complain about her conduct of his case. It was a subtle way of applying pressure by letting Dr. Kelsey know that Merrell had access to much more important people in the FDA.

On the thirty-first of January, Dr. Murray called Dr. Smith again and asked if he had "anything to report." Dr. Smith had spoken to Dr. Kelsey by this time and told Murray he was afraid there was much more to review than the wording of the label. Murray was upset. He said Merrell would have to postpone their schedule for marketing the drug. On February 1, Murray completed his month of pressure tactics by telephoning Dr. Kelsey to tell her that Merrell planned to release the drug for marketing on March 6 and wanted to get the labels printed. Dr. Kelsey remained as calm—and as immovable—as a rock. She told Dr. Murray that the drug would be marketed only when she approved it and that approval would only come when she received an application with completely satisfying scientific data in it.

Meanwhile, in Europe, two executives of Chemie Grünenthal had made a flying visit to England. British doctors had been reporting a number of cases of polyneuritis, and the British licensee for the drug, Distillers, Incorporated, decided to put a warning about the side effect on their labels. The German executives were very upset by this decision. "The open reference to polyneuritis in view of the world-wide importance of K-17 [their code name for thalidomide] is not at all to our taste," they declared. After all, the drug was being considered by the FDA in the United States.

Back in the United States, Dr. Kelsey picked up a copy of the *British Medical Journal* of December 31, 1960. In it was a letter from a doctor in Scotland, entitled, "Is Thalidomide To Blame?" The doctor reported four cases of polyneuritis and other side effects in patients who had taken the drug. Two to three months later, the patients were still showing nerve damage in spite of the fact that they had stopped taking the drug.

At this point, the long struggle for equality and opportunity waged by American women reached a dramatic climax in the mind and spirit of Frances Kelsey. She had the self-confidence that comes naturally to any person—man or woman—who has achieved a place in his or her profession. She had the training that Elizabeth Blackwell and other pioneer women doctors had wandered the world to win— training that enabled her to evaluate this otherwise baffling scientific report. She instantly remembered the study of the effect of quinine on pregnant rabbits which she and her husband had made in Chicago during World War II. Thalidomide was a lot more powerful than quinine. If the drug could cause damage to adult nerve tissue, a relatively tough substance, it might cause much greater damage to the delicate growing tissues of a fetus, particularly in its first weeks in the womb.

When Dr. Murray tried to resume his pressure game, Dr. Kelsey asked him why he had not told her about the clinical reports of polyneuritis in England. She refused to approve the drug until Merrell could explain these reports. Rather lamely, Murray admitted that he and others at Merrell had read these reports, but the English company had merely put a warning about nerve damage in the brochures they were sending out with the drug. Why couldn't Merrell do the same thing?

It might satisfy the British, but it did not satisfy Frances Kelsey. She told Murray that such a procedure "would not be enough" to get her approval. Instead, she stunned Murray by demanding "complete autopsy reports" of experiments on animals who had received the drug for at least one year. She also demanded a complete list of investigators to whom the company had given the drug for experiments on humans so she could find out whether American users had also contracted polyneuritis.

This new request prompted Dr. Murray to put in a transatlantic phone call to Chemie Grünenthal. He told them that the Merrell Company was going to discuss with the FDA the idea of inserting a warning against polyneuritis in their brochures. The Grünenthal executive smoothly agreed to this concession. He did not tell Murray a word about any cases of polyneuritis in Germany—although by this time the company had accumulated data on over four hundred. Dr. Murray and another Merrell executive flew to England and Germany to confer with representatives of the Distillers Company and Grünenthal. The British gave them a detailed account of new toxicity investigations. The Germans told them as little as possible. Instead of four hundred cases of polyneuritis, Grünenthal admitted knowledge of only thirty-four in West Germany.

Back in America, Merrell found their investigators also were reporting cases of polyneuritis. On March 30, Dr.

Murray visited Dr. Kelsey and admitted that prolonged use of the drug could cause "nervous symptoms," but he insisted that they were infrequent and rapidly reversible as soon as the drug was discontinued. He pressed Dr. Kelsey for a verbal commitment that she would give her approval if the company agreed to put a warning on the drug's label. Dr. Kelsey shook her head. She pointed out that they were only talking about a sleeping pill. It was not a cure for some hitherto incurable disease from which people were dying daily. As she saw it, giving Merrell a license to make people sick would be inexcusable.

"I had the feeling throughout this interview that they were at no time being wholly frank with me and that this attitude obtained in all our conferences regarding the drug," Dr. Kelsey wrote in a memorandum of her conversation with Murray. Later that day, Dr. Kelsey wrote another letter to Merrell, informing them that their application was again considered withdrawn—giving her another sixty days to continue her struggle.

Once more Dr. Murray resorted to over-the-head tactics, visiting Dr. Smith to express "concern" about the delay in granting Merrell's application. On the fifth of April, Merrell sent in new data and bluntly suggested that their proof of the safety of the drug was now more than adequate. They asked Dr. Kelsey to let them know her favorable decision "by telephone as soon as possible." Twice in the month of April, Murray phoned Dr. Smith to complain. He implied that he was in danger of losing his job. He demanded a "yes or no decision." Finally, he announced that a Merrell vice-president was planning to see the Food and Drug Commissioner, George P. Larrick.

Merrell next submitted a letter arguing that many barbiturates currently in use had toxic side effects. They

were trying to make Frances Kelsey look like a meddlesome
fool. On May 5, they got a letter from her which made them
realize that they had badly underestimated their adversary.

> In our opinion the application as it now stands is
> entirely inadequate to establish the safety of Kevadon
> tablets under the proposed labeling. In particular the ap-
> plication does not include complete reports of adequate
> animal studies nor sufficiently extensive complete and ade-
> quate clinical [human] studies to permit an evaluation of
> the toxic effects of the drug. . . . In this connection, we
> are much concerned that apparently evidence with respect to
> the evidence of peripheral neuritis in England was known
> to you but not forthrightly disclosed in the application.

Dr. Murray was on the phone to Dr. Smith four days
after Dr. Kelsey wrote this letter, sputtering that it was
"somewhat libelous." Another threat. Now they were not
merely trying to get Frances Kelsey fired, they were implying
that they would drag her name and reputation through the
law courts. Even if they did not win their case, they might
ruin her career and would certainly subject her to terrible
mental stress. With studied nastiness, Dr. Murray asked Dr.
Smith whether Merrell was being forced to deal only with Dr.
Kelsey. If so, he wondered whether her letter was subject
to "reconsideration." Dr. Smith said the letter came from
the FDA. But he offered to reconsider it if the company
could give him "sufficient reason" to do so.

By this time, Frances Kelsey was starting to feel the
pressure. She was forced to consult an attorney about the
threat of a lawsuit. She spent her nights with Merrell reports
spread across her dining room table, trying from their incomplete data to find out just how thalidomide worked in the human body. Fortunately, she had as a built-in advisor one of the
best pharmacologists in the country, her husband, Dr. Fremont Kelsey. He gave her unqualified scientific support in

her skepticism about Merrell's data. She also sought and received shrewd advice from Dr. Barbara Moulton on how to deal with the office politicians of the FDA.

But a friend, even a husband, can only do so much. Each day, Frances Kelsey had to fight the battle in her office, alone. Merrell continued to apply pressure. On the tenth of May, Murray and another Merrell executive visited Dr. William Kessenich, chief of the Medical Division of the FDA. They made sure that Frances Kelsey knew about their visit. Dr. Kessenich set up a meeting on the following day with Dr. Smith and Dr. Kelsey. In the presence of her two superiors, Frances Kelsey remained adamant. She reiterated her concern about the drug's side effects and said there was "special need" for evidence that pregnant women could take the drug safely. This was a new idea to Dr. Murray. It apparently stopped him in midsentence.

A certain amount of humility appeared in Dr. Murray's next contacts with the FDA. He wrote a letter to Dr. Kessenich promising to complete Merrell's application "as requested by Dr. Kelsey." By the end of May, he was bringing in new data supposedly proving that the drug would not harm unborn babies. The studies were carried out by Dr. Ray O. Nulsen, of Cincinnati, Ohio. No one gave Frances Kelsey any information on Dr. Nulsen or how he operated. This (as with many other facts in this account) only emerged when Dr. Nulsen was forced to testify in legal suits.

Dr. Nulsen had no training in obstetrics. He wrote an article in the June, 1961, issue of the *American Journal of Obstetrics and Gynecology* which Merrell used extensively in its sales promotion. The article said Kevadon had no ill effects on babies delivered of some eighty-one women who had taken it in the last three months of pregnancy. Under later cross-examination, Dr. Nulsen admitted that he did not even write the article. It had been written by Dr. Raymond

C. Pogge, the director of Merrell's Department of Medical Research. Nulsen admitted that he had never seen many of the references cited in the article. He did not even keep a detailed record of the number of pills he had received from Merrell or how many he gave his patients. Asked if he had any records of the reports he sent in, Dr. Nulsen replied, "No, it was all verbal." He gave his information to Dr. Pogge "by telephone, or it may have been that we had lunch together, or it may have been when we played golf."

The study, in short, was an almost total fake. Yet Dr. Murray presented it to Dr. Kelsey as new clinical data proving that Kevadon was safe for the unborn. Thanks to the depth of her experience in pharmacology, Dr. Kelsey was unimpressed, even though she did not know the full story of the study's phoniness. She pointed out to Dr. Murray that it only dealt with women who had taken the drug for the last three months of pregnancy. The fetus was most sensitive to strong drugs in the first three months. On July 26, 1961, Merrell got another letter from Dr. Kelsey informing them that she was requesting a new application with better data.

Another sixty-day struggle began. By this time the thalidomide file had grown to four thick volumes, each the size of a metropolitan phone book. On August 10, Murray telephoned Dr. Kelsey to urge her to meet him and a group of clinical investigators at a Washington hotel. She informed Dr. Kessenich of this strange suggestion. He told Murray that the investigators had better meet in the FDA offices. On the seventh of September, after three more telephone calls to puff up the importance of the meeting, it took place—and laid a giant egg, as far as Merrell was concerned. Under questioning from Dr. Kelsey, one of the clinical investigators admitted that he had seen a case of polyneuritis that was still not cured a year after he had discontinued Kevadon. None of the clinicians had any information on what the drug might do to the fetus. On the attack, Frances Kelsey asked for detailed reports of the polyneuritis cases. She became more and more alarmed as additional cases were brought to her attention.

In Europe, Chemie Grünenthal was fighting a growing number of doctors who were damning thalidomide for causing polyneuritis and forbidding its use in their hospitals. In desperation, they persuaded the Swedish company that was reeling under similar reports to leak a story to the Swedish press claiming that Dr. Frances Kelsey of the FDA was on the point of approving its use in America.

By now, however, polyneuritis was the least of Grünenthal's worries. Throughout Germany, extraordinary numbers of women were giving birth to horribly deformed children. Their arms were so stunted, their hands seemed to project almost directly from their shoulders like the flippers of a seal. Some had no legs. Others had disfigured faces. Because most of the malformations were in the arms, the doctors called it phocomelia from the Greek words *phoke,* seal, and *melos,* limb. Hitherto, the deformity had been so rare that most doctors, even obstetricians, never saw a single case in their entire lives. In September, 1961, a doctor reported twenty-seven cases in the Kiel area alone.

German doctors were baffled. At first they suspected radioactivity, a detergent, or a strange new virus. But another doctor, studying the histories of the stricken mothers of the deformed children, found one drug common to all the cases: thalidomide. When he announced his suspicions, Chemie Grünenthal sent three doctors to visit him, demanding to see his material and threatening to sue him. The doctor's case was irrefutable. All his data had been drawn from hospital records proving that the women had received thalidomide during the early months of pregnancy. Nevertheless, the Grünenthal people accused the doctor of "murdering a drug by spreading rumor." They issued 66,957 copies of a sales promotion leaflet which declared, "Contergan [their trade name] is a safe drug."

In America, Dr. Murray was putting the pressure on Dr. Kelsey again. In late September, ignoring the nonresults of his big meeting, he called Dr. Smith and informed him that Merrell wanted to put the drug on the market by the middle of November and would need to start printing labels early in October. When would they get an approval? Dr. Smith switched Murray to Dr. Kelsey. He tried to get her to set a deadline for a decision and wondered if he could give labeling changes to her on the telephone so that printing could begin in October and the drug could be on the market by Christmas.

Dr. Kelsey said no.

Throughout the month of October, Merrell continued to send in new data and discuss labeling. Dr. Kelsey continued to find the data unsatisfactory and on November 7 wrote another "application withdrawn" letter, starting another sixty-day cycle. The struggle was now entering its fourteenth month. On the thirtieth of November, a much more humble Dr. Murray called Dr. Kelsey to tell her that the drug had been withdrawn from sale in Germany because of reports of abnormal babies born to women who took it early in pregnancy. Murray said he hoped the abnormal births would prove to be "coincidental."

Dr. Kelsey urgently pointed out to Dr. Murray that the company had distributed the drug experimentally to numerous doctors as a cure for morning sickness. She told him to warn these doctors immediately about this awful news from Europe.

Chemie Grünenthal had buckled under fierce pressure from the German government and withdrawn thalidomide from the market. They continued to deny it had anything to do with the deformed children. But evidence was coming their way from the other side of the world. Dr. William G. McBride, a thirty-two-year-old physician from Sydney, Australia, published an article in the British medical journal, *Lancet,* on December 16, 1961, reporting an outbreak of phocomelia in his country, which he had traced to thalidomide. British doctors began reporting an even larger outbreak of deformities in newborn babies from the same tragic cause: the mothers had taken thalidomide. In the next months, the number of deformed babies multiplied around the world to a staggering ten thousand.

It slowly dawned on a stunned American public as they read the stories and saw the horrible pictures in their newspapers that one gallant woman doctor had stood between them and a repetition of this disaster in the United States. As for Frances Kelsey, she was too busy worrying about another aspect of the problem to think about praise. Merrell had given her the impression that only sixty doctors were conducting experiments with Kevadon. Not until the true nature of the drug became obvious did the company admit they had "experimentally" distributed 2,528,412 tablets to 1,267 doctors. FDA agents turned up thirty-six additional doctors who were not participating in the experiment but nevertheless were giving thalidomide to their patients. Dr. Kelsey urgently pressed Merrell to notify every doctor on its list of experimenters about the drug's dangers.

She saw to it that FDA inspectors visited every one of these doctors to pick up remaining supplies of the drug and to inquire whether any pregnant women had received the drug, and if so, what was the outcome of the pregnancy. Nine cases of deformed infants came to light. Another 7 cases were identified in which the mother had received the drug from abroad. There may have been others. Some 410 of Merrell's doctors had kept no records of patients who received the drug. They had been lulled by the assurances of Merrell's brochure, congratulating them on being among the first doctors to use this thoroughly safe drug.

When Senator Jacob Javits, Senator Hubert Humphrey, and other members of the Kefauver committee began conducting hearings on the thalidomide disaster, they asked Dr. Kelsey's boss, Food and Drug Commissioner George P. Larrick, some tough questions. He was forced to confess that as late as August, 1962, almost a full year after the thalidomide scandal had exploded, some of the drug was still in circulation. The committee was shocked to hear that under the law as it then existed, the agency had no authority to prevent a company from distributing a drug far and wide in the so-called "experimental" phase. Senator Humphrey, as an ex-pharmacist, was even more outraged because the drug companies "almost completely ignored certain long-standing evidence to the effect that chemical agents can cause injury to babies in their mothers' wombs."

The senators also spent a lot of time expressing their own and the country's gratitude to Dr. Frances O. Kelsey. The day that she testified was the second anniversary of her arrival at the FDA. Senator Humphrey wished her a happy anniversary. "We are surely happy you are here—and that you were there," he said.

Senator Estes Kefauver, with the approval of his fellow senators, nominated her for the gold medal known as the President's Award for Distinguished Federal Civilian Service. It is interesting to note that no one in the FDA had nominated her.

On August 7, President John F. Kennedy hung the Distinguished Federal Civilian Service Medal around Frances Kelsey's neck. Among the small group of guests she had invited to this ceremony were Dr. Barbara Moulton and

Dr. E. M. K. Geiling. It was Frances Kelsey's way of saying that she had not won her victory alone.

President Kennedy congratulated her for defending "the hopes that all of us have for our children." A few days later, the President announced that he had recommended a "twenty-five percent increase in the Food and Drug Administration's staff, the largest single increase in the agency's history," and the full amount "had been voted by conferees in both houses of Congress." Most important, Congress added some amendments to the drug law to close loopholes through which, in Senator Karl Mundt's words, "you could drive a South Dakota wagonload of hay."

The new law required drug companies to submit to the FDA enough research to guarantee the safety of a drug before it could be tested on humans. No longer would the manufacturers be able to distribute several million pills, virtually putting a drug on the market under the banner of experimentation. A new section of the FDA was created to handle these applications for permission to experiment. Dr. Frances Oldham Kelsey was put in charge of it. As this book went to press, she was still on the job, handling some four hundred applications a year in her same unflappable style. I find that a very comforting fact.

One writer summed up Frances Kelsey's achievement pretty well at the time: "She followed a tradition that only seems new—that of the reasoning woman." I would add to that another tradition which will, I hope, no longer seem new to the readers of this book: woman of courage.

Part V

The Future of Courage

When I first announced that I planned to write a book about American women, I was inundated with suggestions about which ones to choose. Several of my friends pushed for Abigail Adams; others favored Harriet Beecher Stowe; still others insisted that the book would not be complete without a chapter on Frances Perkins. The list went on and on. It included women as diverse as Pocahontas and Jane Addams, Emily Dickinson and Margaret Sanger, Dorothea Dix and Sojourner Truth, Helen Keller and my own mother, Bess Truman.

All of these women deserve a prominent place in our history. Most of them have every right to be called women of courage. At the same time, everyone's perception of courage is different. I realize that some of my readers may disagree with my choices. The twelve women in this book are the ones to whom I responded with admiration and enthusiasm. They are also women who broadened my understanding of courage.

Before I started my research I was under the impression that there was a select group of people who had a unique capacity for physical or moral heroism. Through some dramatic accident of fate, this innate heroism leaped into action and made history. By the time I finished the book, I decided that courage is neither as unique nor as accidental as I had supposed.

Almost everyone has the capacity to be courageous. There was little in Dolley Madison's past life to indicate that she would perform so valiantly in a military crisis. Margaret Chase Smith, an astute and cautious politician, surprised everyone—including herself—when she stood up in the Senate to condemn McCarthyism.

It is true that several of the women in this book only revealed their courage when they were faced with an extraordinary situation. A few, like Mary Harris Jones and Ida Wells-Barnett, made courage a way of life. But at least one, Dr. Frances Kelsey, was not consciously acting out of a wish or intention to be courageous. Her central determination was to do her job, to fulfill her obligations as a scientist and a public servant.

My study of women of courage has taught me that the simplest and most accurate definition of courage is the one offered by Ralph Waldo Emerson: equality to the problem before us. Still unanswered, however, is the question that has tantalized every writer who has examined the anatomy of courage. What makes people equal to the problem before them?

I have tried to get at some of the reasons, but in every case I glimpsed other motives. The energy that Kate Barnard poured into her political career may well have been triggered by a desire to please and impress a father who had never paid her enough attention. Perhaps, as her adversaries charged, Susan B. Anthony really was unhappy about being an old maid. Would either fact make their ordeals less poignant or their goals less praiseworthy?

One of the central themes of this book has been the

evolution of feminine courage from the physical confrontation of danger to the highest and loneliest levels of moral challenge. I have not presented my heroines in chronological order, but there is, I believe, a certain amount of chronology in the varieties of courage they displayed.

Courage in a crisis, that spontaneously brave reaction to a physical threat, was more apt to be needed when the country was in its infancy. Most of the challenges on a frontier, in a war, are bound to be physical. Where the population density was seldom more than one hundred people to a square mile, and often a lot less, the individual woman had to rely largely on herself. A tradition of daring, of endurance, of self-reliance that blended the physical and the spiritual, was an almost inevitable result.

As the nation grew, the opportunities for physical courage diminished and the personal commitment—affection for a father, devotion to a husband, concern for that extended image of a family, the tribe—had to be widened into a more general sense of responsibility for the national good. The women who set out to improve America's moral health were nevertheless inspired by individual loyalties. Prudence Crandall was angered by Canterbury's rejection of her first black student, Sarah Harris. Ida Wells-Barnett was searching for a way to avenge the death of her young friend, Tommie Moss. Mary Harris Jones was haunted by the memory of her underpaid and overworked immigrant father and husband and by the contrast between their lives and the lives of the rich Chicagoans she encountered after her husband's death.

Over the years, the need for moral courage became more urgent, and American women began to think in terms of larger ideas and goals. By then, it had also become apparent that courage had to be extended not only in scope but in time. It had to become fortitude.

Elizabeth Blackwell's long fight to be accepted by the

medical profession, Susan B. Anthony's even longer struggle to win the vote are notable in themselves. But they also illuminate an aspect of courage that is often overlooked by today's impatient young crusaders, who are determined to remake the world overnight. Some battles can be won by a single, courageous act. Others take time, determination, and grit.

It would be unfair to claim that any one of the types of courage I've written about is superior to the others. But if I had to select the one that intrigues me most, I would choose gallantry. This, to me, is a major step in the evolution of feminine courage.

The women who sought justice for the victims of prejudice and greed and the women who showed fortitude in the pursuit of their goals had the ability to communicate their spirit to others and to attract followers to their causes. The women who showed gallantry, like the women who displayed courage in crises, had to stand alone. The wheel of courage had come full circle. American women once more proved that courage, as an individual quality of the mind and heart, depends far more on character and conscience than it does on sex.

When I was writing about some of my favorite examples of feminine gallantry, Kate Barnard, Margaret Chase Smith, and Frances Kelsey, I could not help thinking of that old saying about the loudest critics of the establishment often losing their voices once they get into the power structure. Each of these three women refutes that cynical theory. All rose to positions of influence, but instead of lowering their voices and knuckling under to establishment opinion, they used their offices to fight for their personal ideals and principles.

Looking back over the almost two hundred years between Susan Livingston and Frances Kelsey, I cannot help being proud of the progress women have made in their struggle for equality. Dolley Madison would have given five or six or her best ball gowns for the freedom of political action that Margaret Chase Smith exercised.

But there are discouraging notes, too. The conflict that drove Prudence Crandall out of Connecticut in 1833 was the same one that barred Marian Anderson from Constitution Hall 109 years later. Prejudice is not the only evil that refuses to die. Kate Barnard in her efforts to win justice for Indian orphans was up against the same combination of corruption and indifference that Frances Kelsey had to face in her office at the FDA.

There is a tremendous amount of work still to be done by contemporary women of courage. Not many of us will have the opportunity to emulate the women in this book in a literal way. Only a minority of women can match the scientific talent of an Elizabeth Blackwell or a Frances Kelsey. Fewer still can hope to reach that summit of political power, the United States Senate. But there may come a time when we can demonstrate the same kind, if not the same degree, of courage on a smaller scale.

Only a few of the women I've written about were courageous all their lives. When the Revolution ended, Susan Livingston married a prominent lawyer, moved to Ohio, and concentrated on being a wife and mother. Marian Anderson, after her concert at the Lincoln Memorial, went back to performing on more conventional platforms for purely musical purposes. When I visited Dr. Kelsey in her Food and Drug Administration office, she was calmly processing new drug applications without any trace of the tension and high drama that had surrounded the thalidomide episode.

Courage does not have to be constant, but I would like to see it become contagious. Whether the injustices we fight are public or private, whether we seek excellence in a career or in the home, whether we aspire to influence the thinking of the entire country or just the few people gathered around our dinner tables, I would like to see American women bear witness to the tradition of feminine courage that I have traced in this book.

There is a widespread impression among too many women that they have been left out of the mainstream of American life. Even historians have been inclined to see the courageous women of the past as isolated examples rather than as upholders of a long and proud tradition. This is a serious underestimation of the part women have played in building America. Almost all of the women in this book were involved, to a greater or lesser extent, in major movements in American history. Almost all of them were fighting to carry out basic principles on which this nation was founded.

Perhaps this book, by bringing their accomplishments into focus, will provide inspiration and example for any woman who believes as I do that equal rights imply equal responsibilities.

I hope that men as well as women will read this book. The sooner men realize that women deserve a place of honor in our past, the easier it will be for them to accept women as full-fledged partners in our future.

If men can admit the reality of women of courage, it seems to me that the battle of the sexes is on its way to being over. Women have already demonstrated their equality in intelligence, creativity, and physical stamina. Once courage joins the list, we can abandon that pointless argument over which sex is superior and begin an era of genuine partnership.

Wherever or whenever women demonstrate their courage in the years ahead, I hope it will be different in one detail from the courage displayed by the women in this book. As the final stage in the evolution of courage, I would like to see women's courage *shared* with men of equal courage.

This sharing spirit is the real heart of equality. It is the direction American men and women must take if we are to survive the coming decades. All around us we have sensed a shift in values in recent years. The old, basically masculine, individualism of the frontier and the Horatio Alger age of American business have pretty much expired and with them a lot of other ideas—the perpetual emphasis on competition and growth, the viability of goals built around power and money. No one is quite sure what shape the new values will take, but if this spirit of shared courage takes root, I think we may yet see a new flowering of America, based on the strangely neglected idea of community.

It is an idea as old as the Pilgrims. It was lost, I think, in the vastness of our American space. But now that we have filled that space, it has become crucial for us to live together in an atmosphere of mutual respect and genuine sharing. I cannot think of a better basis for this respect than courage. Nor can I imagine a better way to bring American men and women together to fight for the values of a true community, whether it be against the greed of the few or the apathy of the many, than to remind them that they share a heritage of courage.

Index